ART AND HIS'
OF
SEVILLE

Text by

JOSE MARIA DE MENA

BONECHI

THE ART AND HISTORY OF SEVILLE
Text by JOSE MARIA DE MENA (University Professor at the Royal Academy of History and Fine Arts of San Fernando).

© Copyright   by CASA EDITRICE BONECHI
Via Cairoli, 18/b – 50131 Florence, Italy
Tel.(55)576841/2
Fax (55)5000766

Printed in Italy by
Centro Stampa Editoriale Bonechi.

Translated by: *Amanda Mazzinghi,* Studio Comunicare,
Florence.

ISBN 88-7009-851-6

CREDITS

Foto Arenas: pp. 69-71, 103.

Photographs from the Archives of Casa Editrice Bonechi,
taken by:

Antonio Pérez González: pp. 14, 16, 30, 31b/d, 48-49, 51b, 56b,
58,-59, 61, 62b, 63b, 66a, 67b/c, 68, 74-78, 79a, 84b, 85-86, 87b,
88b/c, 89, 91-97, 102b, 105b, 106, 107a, 108-109, 113-118, 120,
121a.

Luigi di Giovine: pp. 12, 15, 18-19, 20a, 22a, 25-29, 30a, 31a/c,
33-43, 46-47, 50, 52-53, 54b,62a, 63a, 80, 82, 98, 100-101, 104,
105a, 122a, 124-125.

Paolo Giambone: pp. 8-9, 11, 17, 20b, 21, 22b, 23-24, 32, 44-45,
51a, 54a, 55a/b, 56a, 60,64-65,66b, 67a, 72, 79b, 81, 83, 84, 87a,
88a, 99, 102a, 107b, 121b, 123.

Fernández Ordóñez: p. 113b.

THE HISTORY OF THE CITY

THE ORIGINS OF SEVILLE

Seville is considered one of the most important cities of Western Europe because of its millenary inheritance and the variety and greatness of its monuments.
Its origins date back to the Neolitic age.

The Phoenicians: historically Seville dates back to the Phoenician period. Many remains, including the name of the city itself, the Phoenician HISPALIS which through phonetical changes changed into ISPALIS, IXBILIA and finally SEVILLE, bear witness of its Phoenician origins. Most of the small statues and tools, now exhibited in the Municipal Archaeological Museum, belong to this period, including the famous bronze statue of the goddess Isis-Astartis, on whose pedistal the following inscription can be read (translated by Professor P.J. Ferron of the Museum of Carthage): "OFFER DONE BY B'LYTN, SON OF D'MIK SON OF D'MIK, TO THANK OUR GRACIOUS GODDESS ASTARTE-HORUS FOR LISTENING TO OUR PRAYERS".

The Tartesses: this civilisation, which flourished during the Phoenician domination, or perhaps earlier still, achieved its acme between the 8th and the 6th century B.C.
The famous treasure of El Carambolo dates back to the hey days of this civilisation; it consists in diadems, some armours, a necklace, a belt and some bracelets which probably were part of the official outfit of a king or may be a priestess, now exhibited in the Archaeological Museum.

The Greeks: some historians believe that one of the frequent Greek expeditions to Spain reached the capital of the Tartesses, situated near the river Baitis (Betis, Guadalquivir), near the lagoon of Lagustina (a marsh land – marismas – which originally extended as far as Seville).
All this information enables us to identify the ancient Tartessian capital with Seville.
The first Greek expedition was commanded by Kolaios of Samus, a famous navigator quoted by Herodotus. The king of the Tartesses, Argantonius, thought that a relationship with the Greeks would have favourably influenced his civilisation and would have prevented the Phoenicians from exploiting them. He therefore tried to convince Kolaios of Samus to settle a commercial and trade centre in Seville by overwhelming him with gifts. The Greeks, however, never settled in the area and limited themselves to sporadic commercial expeditions.

The Carthaginians: around the 6th century B.C. the Carthaginians, a "creole" branch of a Phoenician tribe, resulting from the union of Phoenicians and North-African populations, aware of their power decided to gradually take possession of the whole of Spain. The arrival of the Carthaginians in Seville marks a new phase in the history of the city. During the Phoenician domination it was a flourishing commercial centre but now, with the Carthaginians, the trades grew considerably. In fact most of the minerals, metals and manufactures were all exported to Carthage and its dominions. In 238 B.C., with the First Punic War, the rivalry between Rome and Carthage broke out. The commander Hamilcar Barca, summoned by the Carthaginian Senatus, crossed the straits of Gibraltar and conquered Cadiz. Proceeding along the Guadalquivir river he took possession of Seville which attempted to hold out against the military occupation. The Tartesses, who were governors and allies of Carthage, now became the defeated and the slaves.
The war between Carthage and Rome extended also to these territories. After more than twenty years of battles and military campaigns, during the Punic Wars period, the Romans finally established in the Bethic region, better known as Andalusia, submitting Jaen, where the famous Carthaginian general Hannon was sent to Rome in fetters with 300 of his dignitaries.
In 206 B.C. Publius Cornelius Scipio defeated the Carthaginians in Córdoba.
When the news of the defeat spread, the commander Asdrubalis and Mago, the son of Hamilcar Barca, gathered together the survivors of the fleeing Carthaginian army. They recruited new troops and gathered together an army of more than 450,000 cavalrymen and 50,000 foot soldiers to defend Seville against Scipion. The battle took place near the city, in a place called Ilipa (now Cortijo de Repla). The Carthaginians were defeated and fled towards Cadiz where they were destroyed in the marshes.
Scipio conquered Seville and overcame the Carthaginians. The city was plundered and burnt and some of the remains of palisades and the house, recently discovered by archeologists in calle Sierpes when the Cinema Imperial was built, can still be seen.

Seville was rebuilt soon after and made into a large and more functional city. It the years that followed the Forum, the Porticos, the Baths and several commercial wharfs, recently found in calle Méndez Nunez and in Plaza Nueva, were built on the site of the river bed.

During the first years of the Roman domination, the military campus of Seville consisted in an *oppidum* which was situated where now calle Augusto Placencia stands. Some years later, after the civil war between Caesar and Pompey, the survivors of Pompey's arm, who were defeated in Pharsalia, moved to Spain taking refuge in Seville. Caesar reached Spain in only twenty-seven days and defeated Pompey's soldiers definitely in the battle of Munda, a village near Seville. From there he turned to the capital, which was defended by Pompey's soldiers and by their supporters. The city was soon forced to surrender to the power of Caesar's army, who executed all Pompey's supporters and all his Lusitanian allies. Pompey's head was exposed in the Forum (46 B.C.).

Caesar became lord of the city. He did not limit himself to rebuilding all that had been damaged by the war but ordered the construction of new buildings, streets and a new city wall to defend it from future attacks.

Thanks to these restoration and fortification works he was named Father of the Hispanic nation and infact today his statue can still be admired next to the one of Hercules, the founder of the city, on the Arquillo of the Town Hall and on one of the pillars of the Alameda de Hércules.

In the Roman period Seville was a very rich city. It exported large amounts of wine and corn. This has been clearly witnessed both by the several inscriptions on the tablets found in Seville and on the numerous amphoras and terracotta oil-pots in which goods were transported. The latter were manufactured in Triana, the pottery makers quarter, and were so numerous that the incredible amount of fragments of it originated the so-called "pottery mountain" (*testa* stands for pot), that is Monte Testaccio.

Seville was therefore a very active trading centre: a *negotium*. Next to it was situated the residential quarter or the satellite town of Italica, that is the *otium*. More than 100 quadrigas, litters and horses a day, connected the *otium* to the *negotium*. They were used mainly by rich merchants who lived in the residential centre of Italica to reach Seville and carry out their trades.

Here there were their pantry-houses, their olive storage rooms, oil-presses, from here sailed all the ships which connected the port of Seville with all the ports of the Roman Empire. Italica was built by Scipio the African as *castra valetudinaria*, that is a camp where wounded or sick legionaries could rest. It later became the residential area for patricians. Emperors like Traianus, Adrianus and probably Teodosius were born here. Among its ruins, about 15 km from Seville, there still can be seen the remains of its beautiful architecture, mosaics, statues, a magnificent theatre and outstanding amphitheatre or circus, with its cavae where wild animals were kept and an arena where gladiators fought against Numidian lions and wild bulls from the marismas. That is probably where the bull fights originated from. Its political importance in the Roman Empire is well known.

Emperor Constantine had his code of laws, the so called *Lex cum Servium*, published in Seville, on 18th April 336. This clearly marks the supremacy of this city over all the other Spanish cities. The imposingness of its monuments can be judged upon the height of the columns of one of the most ancient buildings which still can be seen at the beginning of calle Marmoles. Two of the pillars were moved, in the 16th century, to Alameda de Hércules, and they represent today the most admirable examples of the Roman works of arts in Seville.

The Archaelogical Museum exhibits very important works of art which date back to the Roman period: there are several tablets, burial stones, magnificent statues, splendid mosaics which originally decorated the public buildings, palaces and villas of the city, which maintained, because of its noble origins, the ancient name of *Hispalis*.

Later the name was changed in *Julia* in honour of Julius Caesar and because of its similarity to Rome it was later called *Romula*. HISPALIS COLONIA JULIA ROMULENSIS, Salve!

SEVILLE AND THE VISIGOTHS

At the beginning of the 5th century the Germanic tribes who had inhabited the regions of Central Europe, some of which had been ruled by Romans, others had been allied to them by means of agreements, migrated southwards taking advantage of the weakness of the Roman Empire. The Eastern Goths, better known as Ostrogoths (OST-GOTHUM) moved to Italy whereas the Western Goths, the Visigoths (WEST-GOTHUM) migrated to Spain followed by the Swabians, the Vandals and The Halanes.

In 421 Seville surrendered to the Vandals and to their leader Gundericus. After eight years of pillages and devastions which originated the word "vandalism" (which was used to describe a useless and gratuitous destruction), they finally abandoned Seville probably because of the influence of the Swabian and Gothic tribes (429) migrating to Africa where they set up a precarious form of Roman government. In 441 the Swabes, who had finally reached an agreement with the Hispano-romans, took arms against Seville. They behaved very cruelly to the city moreso because the inhabitants were catholics whereas the Swabian tribes followed the priscillanistic heresy. Later the Swabes retired to Galicia leaving Seville to the Visigoths who proclaimed it capital of their new reign. Seville was the seat of the government under the reigns of King Almarcus, Teudi and Teudiselus. The latter, because of his tyrranic behaviour, gave rise to hatred in the noble Sevillian and Visigothic families who, at night during a banquet, murdered the king after blowing all the candles out.

The episode is remembered as the "Supper of the Candles".

Atanagildus, the successor of King Teudiselus, moved his court to Toledo.

In the mean time the Roman-byzantine imperial troops took possession of a large part of Andalusia and governed it from the military camps of Medina, Sidonia and Cadiz.

In 572 King Leovigildus undertook a war against them managing to expell them from his territory. To avoid further invasions he appointed a vice-roy, that is a governor general of the Betic region, and chose his son Hermenegildus. The Visigoths were Arians but the inhabitants of Seville were mainly Catholics. Hermenegildus was convinced by the Bishop of Seville, St. Leandrus, to convert to Catholicism and was baptized in the Cathedral (which at the time was situated on the site of the modern church of St. Julian). The Sevillians acclaimed Hermenegildus who, convinced he was powerful enough, proclaimed himself King of the Visigoths and chose Seville as his capital.

On hearing the news Leovigildus declared war against his own son. He reached Seville with a powerful army. The Sevillians, who had taken refuge within the city wall, trusted in the help of the Byzantines who had settlements in Cartagena and along the north-African coast. In order to avoid them coming into contact with the Byzantines Leovigildus deviated the course of the Guadalquivir, conveying it into a new bed between Seville and Triana so that the Byzantine ships could not come in reach of the city wall.

Unable to oppose the siege, Hermenegildus left the city at night time with twelve cavalrymen and took refuge in the castle of San Juan de Azualfarache where he was captured soon after and taken back to Seville where he was thrown in to the prison which once stood near Puerta de Córdoba. Now there stands a church in his memory which bears his name. Hermenegildus was later taken to Alicante from where he managed to escape and gather a new army in Valencia.

He was taken prisoner once again, condemned to death by Leovigildus and executed in Tarragona.

During the Visigothic reign lived in Seville two famous brothers, both prelates and later declared saints. Leandrus converted Hermenegildus to Catholicism and took part in the III Council of Toledo; he is considered one of the most famous reformers of the Church. It was he who created the "seminars", that is schools in which catholic priests were educated and formed. His brother was even greater. Isidor, who succeeded him to the office of bishop, was the author of the famous *Ethimologies* a sort of compendium of the ancient Roman culture.

The *Ethimologies*, which are an admirable work of art, comprise all the knowledge of the time. The work, divided into twenty volumes, examines different subjects such as: Medicine, Astronomy, Music, Law, Military Art, Geography, Zoology, Architecture, Mineralogy, Theology, Grammar, Rhetorics and many other cultural and scientific subjects. Thanks to St. Isidor the ancient Greco-Roman culture was preserved all through the obscure medieval age.

SEVILLE UNDER THE ARAB DOMINATION

The Visigothic empire ended tragically in 711. There followed a period of fights and contrasts among the several factions who were against Don Rodrigo, guilty of usurpating the throne of Toledo against the legal right of Wutiza's sons. The party of the latter, led by the bishop of Seville Don Oppas, signed an agreement with the Moslem tribes who lived along the north-African coasts, and paid them a large sum of money to send troops in support of Wutiza's sons.

Obviously, as usually happens in these cases, after their victory they refused to leave Spain. Nothwithstanding the fact that Don Oppas had paid the agreed compensation and offered to give them other treasures, the Moslem tribes decided to continue their march through Spain and conquer it.

The Gothic army took refuge in Seville and fought courageously against the Mauritans. Muza Ben Nasair, the commander of the Arab army, not being able to take possession of the city, decided to lay siege on it with a part of his army. His son Abdelaziz Ben Muza surrounded Seville while his lieutenant marched against Toledo and he himself marched towards Mérida.

The Sevillians, short of victuals, were defeated and Abdelaziz conquered the city. He murdered all the dignitaries and occupied the palace of the vice-roy. All the same, in order to avoid a rebellion of the population, he did not dare to go and live in it and chose the Monastery of Santa Rufina as his palace. The monastery was situated just outside the city wall and was a very safe place.

The Arab domination gave rise to struggles for power among the new rulers. Abdelaziz decided to marry Doña Egilona, the widow of the Gothic King Don Rodrigo. But the *Scythians*, distrusting the marriage between an Islamic prince and a Christian, whom they thought would be against the Coranus and aim at restoring the Gothic monarchy, denounced him to the Caliph of Damascus. The latter appointed the cousins of Abdelaziz to kill him in the mosque (716).

In all this period Seville remained the capital of Spain. The Arabs, fearing the population would rebel after Adelaziz's death, preferred to move the capital to Cordoba, which became the seat of the Emirate and later of the Caliphate.

From now onwards, for at least three centuries, Seville followed the same fate as Córdoba, being its province, both during the Emirate and the Caliphate. The Islamic religion soon expanded partly because of the privileges which were given to those Christians who chose to convert to Islamism. Those who refused to do so were overtaxed or persecuted or worse still tortured to death. The few christians who decided to be faithful to their religion were called *Mozarabes*.

The Arabs changed the name of the city to HIMS, name by which the city was known all through the Islamic period. The ancient name of HISPALIS remained popular only among the *Mozarabes* because it represented part of their cultural and linguistic inheritance. That is why Seville had two names, HIMS, which was the official name, and HISPALIS, which underwent phonetical changes and became IXBILIA later SIVILLA and SEVILLA. The name HIMS is still quoted in 1225 by many Islamic texts as for example in *Mu-yam Al-Buldar* by Yaqui al Hamawi.

Among the many important events which took place in this period there must be remembered the arrival of the Normans, better known as Vikings, in 844 during one of their raids in the south of Europe, they came to the mouth of the Guadalquivir. Their ships found no difficulty in sailing up the river to Seville, because of the carelessness of the Islamic garrison. They entered the city and sacked it for over seven days. Finally they retired, laden with treasures and a rich booty of women and slaves, to their ships. The Sevillians soon reacted and together with the Moorish troops, who had swiftly arrived from Córdoba, blocked the retreat to the ships by burning them. The Norman warriors, deprived of their ships, fought for 42 days until they were finally defeated and destroyed in Tablada. The Viking records quote this disaster as the "year in which the fleet never returned".

Another important event in the history of Seville was the rebellion of Omar Ben Hafsum.

Hafsum was a *mowalla*, that is he was of Islamic religion and descendant of one of the noblest Visigothic families, who had been converted to Islamism.

Omar Ben Hafsum, on hearing that the Goths had risen in Asturias, Aragona and Navarra and created Christian reigns decided to do the same in Andalusia. He embraced the Christian religion with all his family and armed his troops retiring to the Bobastro Mountains.

Omar Ben Hafsum occupied large part of Andalusia and all the region south of the border which ran from Almeria to Hueva through Seville. The nearest village to Córdoba was Aguiler de la Frontera. The Caliph of Córdoba, alarmed by these events, mobilized all his troops. Omar Ben Hafsum was honoured with favour – the population in fact resented the Caliphs of Córdoba, who descended from the Caliphs of Damascus, and their government – hoping they could finally proclaim their independence; this explains why the war lasted for over 20 years. All of a sudden the Christian kings of the north and the whole of Europe forsook Omar Ben Hafsum. There is a strange political mystery which explains this strange case. The Christian world left this small Christian reign to fight on its own until it gradually weakened and fell.

The Caliph of Córdoba managed to spur the rebellion of the Yemenites and Berber tribes, who inhabited the northern side of Seville. With the help of the Governor of Seville, the city gates were mysteriously opened. Berbers and Yemenites exterminated the population, sacked the city and finally set fire to it, half-destroying it.

A Yemenite poet wrote this terrible poem:

"With daggers in our hands we have killed
Every single son of a slave.
Their corpses, twenty thousand.
Cover the ground like a carpet.
The others float on
The waters of the Guadalquivir."

Seville, which in the past had reached an economic stability, with a rich patrician class and a middle class made up by merchants, undertakers and active artisans, did not recover until many years later.

In 1035, after the death of Hixen II, Córdoba was the scene of a barbarous court revolt between *Sunnites* and *Shiites* which resulted in the final downfall of the reign.

Mohamed Ben Abbas, the Governor of Seville, however, announced soon after that Hixen II was not dead but that he had been imprisoned in Córdoba, had managed to escape and retire to Calatrava. From there he entered Seville hailed by the population.

We will never know if the person who was appointed as Caliph by the shrewd Ben Abbas was Hixen II himself or a mat-maker who was put in his place. Some governors, however, refused to submit to Córdoba and recognise the authority of the Caliph Huxen II. In reality, though, it was Mohamed Ben Abbas who governed Seville and all the other provinces and therefore created an autonomous reign. The name of Hixen II appears in some official records until it finally disappears. The governor Ben Abbas proclaimed himself King of Seville and his reign took the name of Al-Motahdi.

He soon realised that his reign was endangered by the Berber tribes of Morón and Ronda and by the

Yemenites of Badajoz, so he decided to eliminate them by means of a stratagem.

First he visited the tribes and honoured their sheiks with gifts of all kinds. Then he invited them to Seville with the excuse of celebrating a banquet in honour of the restored peace.

The sheiks arrived at the Sevillian Alcazar where steam baths, cold water swimming pools and a massage parlour had been arranged. The sheiks, who were tired and hot, thanked him for the reception and entered the sauna. Soon after the steam temperature started to increase. Not being able to bear it, they tried to leave the sauna, but the doors were locked so that the 60 Yeminite princes and Berber sheiks died of soffocation.

Al-Motahdi strengthened his power and transformed Sevilla into a military power, the strongest in Spain.

His son gave a touch of refinement to it: scholars from every part of the world flocked here. His wife Itimad, patronized every sort of intellectual activity and in particular poetry, probably because she was a poet herself.

Al-Motahmid enriched the city by building mosques (the present-day church of San Juan de la Palma), palaces (the Monastery of St. Clements), public buildings, gardens and the Great Mosque of Ad Abbas in honour of his father. Some remains of this mosque can still be seen in the Patio de los Naranjos, near the church of San Salvador in Plaza del Salvador.

This love for culture and the close relationships with the western world gave rise to distrust in the *alfaquies*, that is the priests of the Islamic religion, who saw in all this a threat to orthodoxy and to the religious practice, more so because they feared the behaviour of Oueen Imad, who took part in literary meetings, might subvert the social role of women.

In this same period (1084) the King of Castile, Alfonso VI, proposed to marry Zaida, the daughter of Al-Motahmid. Zaida married the king and reigned with the name of Isabel ("Elisabeta Regina" quote the historical records of the time).

But soon after disagreements between father-in-law and son-in-law gave rise to a war. In his turn. Al-Motahmid, ill advised by his *alfaquies* asked for the assistance of the Emperor of Morocco, the Caliph of the Almoravides, Yusuf Ben Texufin.

Yusuf hastened to his aid with a powerful army and defeated the troops of the King of Castile in the battle of Sagrajas. Later, however, Yusuf, taking advantage of the accusations with which the *alfaquies* charged him, imprisoned him and sent him, in fetters, to Morocco, where he died in the prison of Agmat. Yusuf added this reign to his pre-existing empire and in 1091 he transformed it into one of Maghreb's provinces.

Under his domination Seville was fortified; in fact the city wall was enlarged and ran from the Macarena towards Resolana and the present-day calle Torneo, Gravina, Adriano y Arpe, up to calle Santander where it joined with the Alcazar buttress. For greater security the emperor kept a garrison in Seville; this was formed neither by Mauritans nor by Berbers but by black men who came from the southern region of Argelia.

Yusuf transformed the city into a vice-royal capital, which extended its prestige from the river Tajo to Gibraltar and rivalled in stateliness with Marrakesh itself. Yusuf belonged to a fundamentalist religious group and had all books banned except the Koran and had the main libraries in Andalusia publically burnt.

In 1120 the political-religious current of the Almohades (followers of Mehdi) started to threaten the reign of Yusuf. They were far more learned than the Almoravides and Yusuf feared they would join the Christians and *muladies* (Christians who had been converted to Islam). He ordered all the Almohades and the Christians to be persecuted. The latter were represented by the few Mozarab Christians who still lived in Andalusia, that is in Seville, Córdoba and in the villages of these provinces. They were fewer than ten thousand and were forced to flee to Castile and León to avoid persecution.

All the same the Almohade triumphed in Morocco and in 1161 the new Almohade Caliph settled in Seville.

Under the Almohade domination Seville Islamic architecture reached its maximum splendour. The Almohades enriched the city with new mosques, they built a boat bridge to connect the city with Triana and built several other palaces and public baths. The Great Mosque of Ad Abbas, built by Al-Motahmid, proved to be far too small, so the Emperor Abu Yacub had a new mosque built in Seville, which rivalled in beauty the magnificent mosque of Córdoba. Of this mosque there remains only the Patio de los Naranjos with the Pardon Door and the minaret, known as Giralda. Both works were built by the engineer Gever, by the architect Aben Baso and by the superintendent Ali of Gomara, all from Morocco.

As the scholar Tubinus says: "The Almohades furnished Seville with huge monumental buildings". Unfortunately these works proved to have very high costs. To build the Giralda the Almohades used the stones of the ancient Roman buildings. Some of these bore inscriptions of the Augustan age which still can be admired, at ground level, at the foot of the Giralda.

The Almohades built the buttress of the Alcanzar, which strangely enough does not overlook the yard towards where the defence against the external enemies took place, but overlooks the city. Probably it was used in case the population rebelled against the foreign rulers.

The last building which dates back to this period but whose origin dates back to the 13th century, is the Torre del Oro, which was built by the governor Abu Eola.

A view of some architectonical details of the Cathedral.

Some sculptural details of the apse of the Cathedral. ▶

The House of Pilate, an example of ceramic decoration. ▶

THE CHRISTIAN MEDIEVAL AGE

In 1247 the King of Castile and León, Ferdinand III 'The Saint' reconquested Andalusia expelling all the Islamic tribes. He took Jaen and Córdoba, laid siege on Seville and although his army was far less powerful that the Arab troops, after a year of fierce battles they entered the city (victoriously).

St. Ferdinand moved his court to Seville where there continued to live his successors: Alfonso X the 'Wise', Sancho IV, Ferdinand IV, Alfonso XI and Pedro I, known as the 'The Cruel' or 'The Just'. One of St. Ferdinand's sons built in the 13th century the magnificent tower of Don Fadrique which marks the transition from Romanic to Gothic.

Pedro I embellished the city by building several churches in *mudejar* style, such as All Saints' church, St. Mark's church, St. Marina's and St. Catherine's church, whose bell towers resemble the Giralda.

He also built the Alcazar in the same shape we still see it today, in fact only a small part of the ancient Arab Alcazar had remained after the earthquakes in the 14th century. The halls on the ground floor, and in particular the Patio de las Doncellas, the Patio de las Muñecas and the magnificent Hall of the Embassadors, all built during the reign of Pedro who gathered around his court a large number of Islamic and Christian artists for this magnificent palace to be built.

The cathedral was built in the 15th century. The earthquakes had severely damaged the large Almohade Mosque with exclusion of the Patio de los Naranjos and the Giralda Tower. The Capitolum, which met in July 1401, ordered a new cathedral to be built in Gothic style on the site of the ancient mosque: "We shall build such a large church that those who will see it finished will consider us crazy"... In fact the cathedral is the largest in the whole of Europe second, in size, only to, St. Paul's cathedral in London.

At the end of the 15th century, after the discovery of the New Continent, Seville became the maritime capital of the Spanish empire.

EL SIGLO DE ORO

The discovery of the New Continent enriched Seville. In fact in 1503 the Casa de Contratación was created; it was responsible for controlling all the commerce with the colonies also because Seville was the only port from which the ships bound to America could sail. Therefore Seville became the most important trading centre at the time.

There rose a new class of rich merchants who built sumptuous houses and contributed to the building of several monasteries and opulent churches. Artists from all over Spain were called here by the gold and treasures arriving from the New Continent.

Many sumptuous edifices were built in this period such as the House of Pilate, the Town Hall or Ayuntamiento, a masterpiece of Renaissance art, and the Hospital de las Cinco Llagas, one of the largest in the world. The commissary Francisco de Zapata y Cisneros, Count of Barajas, had new doors built in the city wall of which there survives today the Postigo del Aceinte. He also built the Alameda de Hércules, one of the most beautiful promenades in Europe.

Seville also had several universities such as St. Thomas and Santa María del Jesús. They were frequented by many famous authors like Cervantes, Lope de Vega and Tirso de Molina, who wrote many of their comedies in these beautiful Sevillian patios. Famous sculptors and painters such as Torrigiano, Alesio, Mercadante of Brittany, Zurbarán, Pacheco, Martínez Montañéz, Luisa Roldán de Mena known as "La Roldana" competed with worldwide famous artists.

The height of the Sevillian Baroque age was marked by Velázquez and Murillo who were the greatest painters of the period.

THE 18TH CENTURY

The 18th century marks the economical decline of the city. Seville loses its monopoly over trade with the colonies. All the same, its culture was enriched by the contribution of Pablo de Olavide, the commissary of Seville who gave birth to the progressive current known as "La Ilustración".

The Real Fábrica de Tabacos was also built, which, at that time, was the largest civil building in the whole of Spain, now seat of the Hispalense University. The new quarter of Molviedro was built in addition to the Plaza de Toros de la Real Maestranza, a masterpiece of Spanish architecture.

The palace of St. Telmus (used as a college by Navigators) and the church of St. Louis, in Baroque style, were also built in this period.

THE 19TH CENTURY

The century starts off with the War of Independence. The Sevillan artillery captain, Luis Daoiz, is the first hero who fought against Napoleon. For some time Seville was the seat of the Supreme Government Council who directed the whole war. But Seville gradually became impoverished and all the nation was struck by political rebellions. The famous author Duke of Rivas wrote his comedy *Don Alvaro or The Power of Fate*, which will inspire the opera *The Power of Fate*, in Seville, where he had retired. Seville inspired many other works of the Romantic period such as *Carmen, Don Juan, The Barber of Seville, The wedding of Figaro, Alfonso and Estrella* and the unfinished work by Beethoven of which the famous ouverture *Fidelio* is part.

The last years of the 19th century were englightened by the presence of the so called "Small Court" of the infanta Maria Luisa and her husband, Don Antonio of Orleans, Duke of Montpensier who lived in the Palace of San Telmo. Mercedes, the daughter of the Dukes of Montpensier, married Alfonso XII and died at the age of 19 throwing the whole of Spain into mourning. It was in this century that the popular arts reached their acme, that is the corrida with famous *matadors* like Josef Delgado named "Hillo", Antonio Sánchez, named "Teto" and Manuel García named "El Espartero". Flamenco found its natural environment in the *cafè chantants*, such as the Café del Burrero and the Café de la Silvería, which were real temples of flamenco.

THE 20TH CENTURY

In this century Seville undergoes a new economic growth. The *Hispano Aviación* was built in 1918, in addition to the first pavilions for the Hispano-American Fair of 1929. These pavilions were true architectural masterpieces which still can be admired in Plaza de España and Plaza de América in the Park of María Luisa.

Famous architects such as Anibal González, Juan Talavera, José Saez, Gomez Millán and Vincente Traver gave a new architectural look to Seville creating the Sevillian regionalistic style. Many buildings were built for the Fair, one for each country in the architectonical style of the country itself. We can still admire the pavilions of Chile, Colombia, Perú and Guatemala and many more too.

The culture in the 20th century influenced art and literature. The famous symphonic composer Joaquín Turina, who represented the works by Manuel de Falla, was born here. The Betic Orchestra was created. Seville was the birthplace of poets such as Manuel Machado, Antonio Machado and Vicente Aleixandre who won the Nobel. Pedro Nuñoz Seca, Pedro Pérez Fernández and the Alvárez brothers representend here most of their comedies. Painters like Gonzalo Bilbao and Alonso Grosso became famous throughout the world.

SEVILLE TODAY

Seville is now busy organising the Universal Exposition to be held in 1992, EXPO-92. For this purpose new motor-ways and highways are being built in addition to viaducts, a new railway station in Santa Justa. The intercontinental airport is being enlarged (Aeropuerto San Pablo) and many new bridges on the Guadalquivir are being built. Palaces, churches and other monuments are being restored. At the beginning of the '70s many political changes took place, the administration was modified and has brought to the creation of regional autonomous governments. Seville is now the capital of the Autonomous Government of Andalusia (installed in the chapel of the ancient college of St. Hermenegildus in Plaza de la Concordia; it will be soon moved to the Hospital de las Cinco Llagas, built in the 16th century after restoration has been completed). The Presidence of the Autonomous Government is now seated in Palacio de los Monsalves but it will soon be removed to the Palace of St. Telmus (the ancient court of the Montpensier's) at the entrance of the Park of María Luisa.

Expo-92 in which more than a hundred countries will take part has required the construction of pavilions for every single nation, of new hotels, commercial centres and public and recreational facilities. A new Opera theatre, an Auditorium, a stadium and many other buildings are also being built. After the International Exposition Fair Seville will be a new city ready to face a new century, 2000, a new millennium with a new life-style full of economical and cultural opportunities.

A building decorated in colours typical of Spanish taste. ▶

TOURING ROUND SEVILLE

The monuments we shall visit are situated, topographically, near the old city centre. This was enclosed by a city wall, which had schematically an oval plan, – "Seville appears like the blade of a sword" – wrote a Medioeval author. The boundaries of the ancient city walls are now marked by the following calles: Puerta de Jérez, Almirante Lobo, Paseo Cristobal Colón, Reyes Católicos, Julio César, Marqués de Paradas, Torneo, Resolana, Puerta de la Macarena, Andueza, Ronda de Capuchinos, Recaredo, Menéndez y Pelayo, San Fernando, ending on the opposite side in Puerta de Jérez.

Two perpendicular lines divide the center into four sections. The former crossed the city from south to north, it starts off in Puerta de Jérez and taking different names such as Avenida de la Constitución, Plaza Nueva, Calle Tetuán, Plaza del Duque, Calle Trajano, Alameda de Hércules, ends in the Resolana, near the Macarena. The latter oriented from west to east starts off in the calle Marqués de Parada and taking different names such as calle Alfonso XII, Plaza del Duque, Campaña, calle Martín Villa, Laraña, Plaza de la Encarnación, Imagen, Almirante Apodaca, Plaza Ponce de León and calle Jauregui ends in calle Recaredo, near the site of the ancient Puerta de Osario.

The four districts which originate are the following:

First district: most of the historical and artistic monuments are concentrated in this district. Here we find the Cathedral, the Alcazar, the Archives of India, the Town Hall, the church of San Salvador, the church of Annunciation, the Hospicio de Venerables and the Barrio de Santa Cruz, the ancient Jews' quarter.

Second district: here we find the Casa de La Moneda, the Hospital de la Santa Caridad, the Torre del Oro, Torre de la Plata, St. Madeleine's Church, the Plaza de Toros de la Real Maestranza and the Provincial Museum of Fine Arts.

Third district: here we find the Church of San Vicente, the Church of San Lorenzo, the Monastery of St. Clara, the Monastery of St. Clements, calle Calatrava, which reminds us of the legend of Don Juan and the Alameda de Hércules Promenade.

Fourth district: here we find the Roman city walls, the Basilica de la Macarena, the Palace de las Dueñas, the towers of Santa Marina and St. Mark, the Church of San Luis, the Monastery of Santa Inés and the Church of St. Catherine.

◀ Two views of the city from the top of the Giralda.

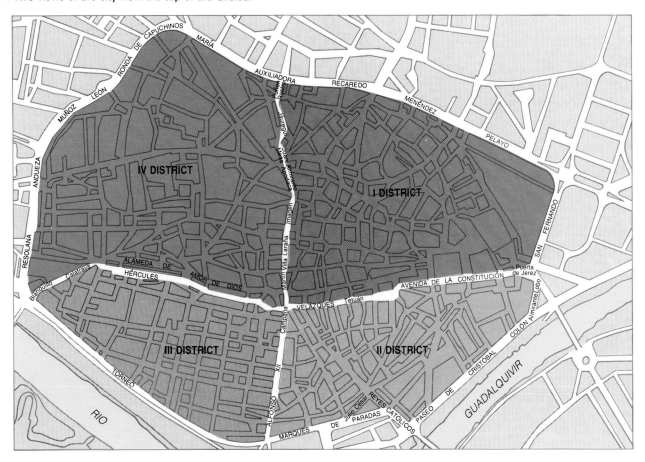

FIRST DISTRICT

Our visit to the city could not but start from this quarter because it is comprehensive of some of the most important and prestigious monuments of Seville, celebrated all over the world.

TOWER OF THE GIRALDA

The cathedral is surrounded by a long row of pillars which delimit all the area up to the church walls, used in medioeval times as a retreat by those who sought asylum.

The building is made up by two different elements; one is an example of Islamic architecture and consists in the Patio de los Naranjos and in the Tower of the Giralda.

In the north-eastern corner of the Patio de los Naranjos stands the *tower of the Giralda*, a minaret of the ancient Moslem mosque. To have a better view of it go back on the road and look at it from the corner of calle Mateos Gago.

The tower is made up by different elements: a Moslem element which was erected in 1184 by the Emperor of Morocco Abu Yacub Yusuf and for which stones of the Roman monuments were used; some of which can still be seen at ground level of calle Placentín. This tower was built by the engineer Gever, who actually built two towers one inside the other. The vacuum space between the two towers houses a flight of steps which was used to reach the upper terrace. That means that the Giralda has no steps except for an ascent which enabled the sultan to go up the tower on his horse. The big decoration was carried out by Aben Baso and by his nephew Ali de Gomaro.

In the 16th century the bell tower was added to the Islamic building, it was built by the architect Hernán Luis of Córdoba. On the top of it you can still admire the lily-shaped element on whose corners stand four bronze pinnacles in the shape of lilies, recently restored by the artist Fernando Marmoleja.

On the top you find different architectonical elements, all of the Renaissance period: the cannons,

◄ A suggestive view of the Giralda.

A view of Plaza de la Virgen de Los Reyes, from the top of the Giralda.

rowels, dome and small dome and on an upper level the gigantic *statue of Faith*, a woman in a classical Roman dress holding a shield in one hand and a palm in the other. According to some authors the statue was designed by Luis de Vargas, modelled by Juan Bautista Vargas the Elder and cast in bronze by Bartolme Morel, it was then placed here in 1568. The statue is movable and that is why it was given the name of Giralda which indicated the "banderol" in the shape of a woman and the tower itself.

From the same corner it is possible to have a magnificent view of the Gothic cathedral, a masterpiece of architecture with its vast raised and rampant arches which discharge the weight on to the ground and on the pillars.

A view of the small dome and the Giraldillo.

Some architectonical details of the Arab minaret.

A particular view of the Giralda. ▶

Two full views of the architectonical complex of the Cathedral, the third biggest church in the Christian world.

THE CATHEDRAL

The cathedral has several doors: the most famous door is *Puerta de los Palos* or of the Adoration of the Magi, on whose spandrel there can be seen the beautiful relief representing the *Adoration of the Magi*, a work by Miguel Florentín (1520). The *Puerta de las Campanillas*, near the main entrance, is also by Florentín. It represents the *arrival of Christ in Jerusalem*. On the opposite side of the building there are another two monumental doors overlooking the Avenida de la Constitución. On their side you can admire six large statues representing the *four evangelists, St. Laureanus and St. Hermenegildus*, all by Pedro Millán.

The interior of the cathedral has five naves; it was designed by Alonso Martínez between 1402 and 1439. The most important element of the church is the *altar piece* on the high altar, considered one of the most important examples of religious art. It was carried out by the Flemish artist Pierre Dankart in 1482. Later other sculptors worked on it until 1564. The altar piece is 18 metres wide and 20 metres high and represents, in 36 large compartments, *episodes of the Old Testament, the life of Christ and of the Saints*.

The *Royal Chapel* is also very sumptuous. Here the *Virgin of the Kings* is venerated, a Gothic image of the French school which is believed to have been given to St. Ferdinand, King of Castile by his cousin St. Louis, King of France. At the foot of the Virgin we find a silver and crystal urn in which it is said the body of St. Ferdinand is buried. The bodies of his wife Beatrice of Swabia, of his son Alfonso X the

From the top of the Giralda one can admire the complex structure of the Cathedral in the form of a cross.

Some details of the rampant arches and some decorative architectonical elements in gothic style.

Above, a full view of the apsidal part of the Cathedral ▶ and the Giralda.
Below, some decorative details of the external apsidal wall of the Cathedral.

The gothic Puerta de los Palos, with the 16th century sculptures by Master Miguel and the lunette with the Adoration of the Magi.

Above, the lunette of Puerta de las Campanillas, with ▶ Christ's arrival in Jerusalem.
Below, Puerta de las Campanillas and another of the splendid carved portals at the sides of the Cathedral.

A particular view of the Cathedral.

The inside of the Cathedral with its very elaborate ▶
gothic ceiling.

Wise are buried in the magnificent arcosolium tombs on both sides of the chapel. Under the altar we find a crypt with a pantheon in which all the kings, queens and infantes of the reign of Castile are buried (12-15th centuries).

There are other famous paintings in the other chapels such as the *Mary Immaculate* by Zurbarán (Chapel of St. Peter), the *allegory of the Conception* by Luis Vargas, also known as "the leg painting" for the perfection with which the leg of Adam has been painted, a *Vision of St. Anthony of Padua* painted by Murillo (St. Anthony Chapel or Baptistery Chapel).

Noteworthy are also the *stained glass windows* of the cathedral, carried out by Master Enrico (1478), others by Mecer Cristobal Alemán (1504) and others by Jean Jacques, Vibán, Bernardino of Gelandia and others.

The *Choir*, with its 117 seats, is also very beautiful. Among the seats there can be admired the royal throne with the coat of alms of the Kings of Castile, those of the prelates and the canons, all works by the sculptor Nufro Sánchez. Noteworthy is also the gigantic lectern used for the books of the Choir.

In the transept we find the *tomb of Fernando*

The altar of the Royal Chapel with the most venerated statue of the Virgin of the Kings.

Head of the transept, near Puerta San Cristobal, ▶ four heralds representing the reigns of Castile, Leon, Aragona ana Navarra, bear the coffin containing the supposedly remains of Christopher Columbus.

◀ A suggestive image of the altar-piece on the high altar in ornate gothic style, the largest in the world with its 220 square metres covered with thousands of figures.

A detail the Nativity represented on the high altar.

One of the internal naves with its strong filleted pillars and the elegant 18th century blue and white jasper floor.
One of the colourful stained glass windows of the Cathedral and the original in bronze of the Giraldillo.

Above, the Main Sacristy in plateresque style and ▶
the large monstrance in silver by Juan de Arfe.
Below, the altar of the Sacristy of the Chalices
with the crucifix by Montañés.

Colombo and next to the Puerta de San Cristobal stands the *burial monument in honour of Christopher Columbus*, whose body was taken from L'Avana to Seville in 1898 when the Spanish domination on the island of Cuba ended. The monument is decorated with four large statues which hold on their shoulders the body of the famous navigator.
The *Capitulary* is also very important because of its magnificent architecture and its vault painted by Murillo.
The Main Sacristy houses the *Museum of the Cathedral*, which exhibits the most precious paintings, the procession monstrances, by the famous goldsmith Juan de Arfe, and other treasures.
Next to the cathedral you can see the Church of the Sagrario famous for its beautiful altars and for its baroque style sculptures.

Two images of the Patio de los Naranjos, the courtyard of the ancient Almohade mosque.

THE PATIO DE LOS NARANJOS

The entrance of the *Patio de los Naranjos* is in calle de Alemanes through the Door of Pardon, which still preserves two beautiful bronze portals with magnificent door knockers, an Almohade work of the 12th century, decorated with ornamental knots and Arab inscriptions.

Almohade style arches enclose the cloister. In the middle of the cloister there can be found a stone fountain which dates back to the Visigoth period. There is also a pulpit from which, at different times, San Vincenzo Ferrer, San Francisco de Borja, San Juan of Avila and other famous orators preached. On the first floor of this patio we find the *Christopher Columbus Library* which preserves a large amount of ancient books and documents which were donated by Don Fernando Colombo, the son of Christopher Columbus.

33

In the ancient walls there is the Door of the Lion, which opens onto the Royal Alcazar.

The Patio de la Montería, so called because it was the meeting place of the King's men, the «Monteros de Espinosa».

A close up of the Patio de las Doncellas, where in ancient times, according to the Arab tradition, public and ceremonial life took place.

THE ALCAZAR

The Alcazar or as it is better known the Royal Alcazar was surrounded by walls. It had two entrance doors which led to two external patios, called the *Flag Patio* and the *Lion's Patio*. We start our visit by entering from the Door of the Lion, on whose architrave there can be admired a heraldic lion in azulejo.

The first hall, on the left, is the *Hall of Justice*; it is decorated in mudéjar style with Islamic plasterwork and the heraldic shields of the Order de las Bandas and of the coats of arms of the Kings of Castile and León.

From here you enter the *Patio de la Montería*, which derives its name from the place where the cavalrymen and the scouts (monteros), who accompanied the king in his hunting parties, met. At the very far end stands the palace of King Pedro I, which was built in 1364. On the façade there is a door with blind arches, and on the upper level one three-fold window in the middle and two two-fold windows on the sides decorate the upper storey. Right in the middle there can be admired a tablet in white and blue azulejo on which you can read the quotation in Arab saying: "There is no winner without Allah". All around there are other Gothic quotations which read as follows: "The greatest, the noblest and most courageous Master Peter, King of Castile and León, had this alcazar and these palaces and these façades built in 1402, by Divine mercy"

On the previous pages, two views of the Patio de las Doncellas with its characteristic lobed arches, azulejos and its polychromous carved ceiling.

The Hall of the Embassadors, richly decorated in Mudejar style, with its dome covered with golden stalactites.

(1364). On the façade there is a jutting gutter supported by a precious trabeation decorated by engravings in moresque style.

Passing through the vast galleries and halls decorated in azulejos tiles and mudéjar ceilings you reach the *Patio de las Doncellas*, which is the main courtyard. The patio is decorated with marble columns and plasters representing moresque style leaves, shields and Christian inscriptions the Moslem motto "Loor a Allah" (Allah is to be praised) is alternated with the motto of Emperor Charles I, "Plus Ultra". This patio is called Patio de las Doncellas, because the ladies of the court used it for their games. The *Hall of the Kings*, the *Hall of Charles V* and the *Hall of the Embassadors* all open onto this patio. The latter is the most important room in all the alcazar and it is considered one of the most beautiful halls in the whole world. The dome, in Moslem style, is by the Sevillian artist Diego Ruiz, who built it in 1389. The dome is covered in metal

mirrors which reflect the light of the whole hall. Among the decorations we find the protraits of the Kings of Spain. On this storey it is worth visiting the *Hall of the Grand Master,* where, according to tradition, the Grand Master don Fadrique, of Santiago, was stabbed to death by his brother Peter I.

We shall now pass to another wing of the alcazar: that is the private residential quarter of King Pedro with the *Patio de las Muñecas*, a small and beautiful patio. All the halls which open onto this patio were inhabited by Pedro and Doña Maria de Padilla, his mistress and later his wife.

All the first storey dates back to the 15th century and was built for the marriage of Emperor Charles I of Spain and V of Germany to Isabel of Portugal.

The tour ends with a visit to the *gardens* in which different styles (Arab, French and Renaissance style) can be admired. Here we find fountains, pools, grottos and a large amount of flowers and plants. Every single corner of these gardens has a particular

40

Two close ups of the Patio de las Muñecas, so called for the female heads carved on the capitals.

The retablo of the Madonna of the Sailors preserved in the Hall of the Admirals.

On the previous pages, two images of the richly decorated Hall of the Embassadors.

name and its own history: the Garden of the Prince, the Garden of the Ladies, the Labyrinth, the Garden of the Dance, etc.

The rooms on the first floor overlook the garden. They were used by Isabel the Catholic, Charles I, Philip V, Isabel II, Alfonso XII, Alfonso XIII, General Francisco Franco and nowadays they are still used by King Juan Carlos and Queen Sofia. The rooms are furnished with furniture of different periods and display numerous pictures and portraits.

The most important room is the *Chapel* or Oratorium of Queen Isabel the Catholic, with its altar in azulejos representing the *Visitation*, a work by the Italian artist Francesco Pisano (1504). Another important hall of the ground floor is the *Hall of the Admirals*, where the expeditions to India were planned, followed by the *Hall of Arras*, where famous Flemish tapestries, representing the conquest of Tunis by Emperor Charles I, are preserved.

Some views of the luxuriant gardens of the Alcazar, which surround the court abodes in accordance with the Arab-Andalusian tradition.

A view of the quarter of Santa Cruz from the top of the Giralda and the Cross of the Cerragería.

Above, the ancient Hospicio de Venerables Sacerdotes ▶ which houses the Museum of the Confraternites, where are exhibited ornaments, models and «pasos» from the processions of Holy Week and a lively and characteristic inn.
Below, the Callejón del Agua.

BARRIO DE SANTA CRUZ

You enter this quarter, an ancient medieval Jews' quarter through the Patio de las Banderas in the Alcazar. The Patio was so called because the Christian banners were put before the military expeditions against the Arabs.
At the end of the patio, on the left, you find a roofed patio known as Patio de la Judería.
It leads to Las Cadenas, a door which connects the buttress of the Alcazar with the quarter of Santa Cruz. The door takes this name from the numerous chains which were used to mark the limits of the asylum retreat.

Some views of the typical quarter of Santa Cruz.

The quarter is a labirynth of narrow and winding alleys with beautiful houses in Sevillian style and wrought iron balconies with flowers, geraniums, carnations, and climbing geraniums. Each house has its own patio closed by a wrought iron gate. The patio which is generally surrounded by columns always has a fountain and flowers. The decoration of the patios can change: there can be paintings, mirrors with chandeliers, ceramic plates and in some cases strut heads of bulls or boars.

Some views of the quarter of Santa Cruz.

Plaza de Doña Elvira. ▶

The church of Santa María La Blanca. ▶

Through the callejón del Agua you reach plaza de Alfaro where, on the left, there can be admired the beautiful balcony of Rosina, one of the main characters of the opera "The Barber of Seville". In calle Lope de Rueda you can admire magnificent medieval façades with ornamental sculptures and heraldic shields. If you proceed along Plaza de Alfaro you find Plaza de Santa Cruz, with the magnificent *Cross of the Cerragería*, a work by the artist Sebastian Conde. The cross, which dates back to the 17th century, gives the name to the square and is situated on the site where once the ancient Church of Santa Cruz stood. The painter Bartolomé Estebán Murillo is buried somewhere under the square, in fact his tomb was in the church which no longer exists.

In the quarter of Santa Cruz, and in particular in calle Santa Teresa, there can be admired the *Convent of Santa Teresa*, founded elsewhere by her in 1576 and moved to this site in 1586. The church is in baroque-style and on its high altar there can be admired a *painting of the Virgin*, a work by Juan de la Mesa.

Other panels on the side altars, represent the *Flagellation and Resurrection of Christ*, the latter is a work by Herrera the Elder. In the Sacristy there are several mementos of St. Theresa of Avila, among which there can be found several letters and the original manuscript of Las Moradas and a portrait of her painted by Juan de la Miseria in 1576.

Returning to the upper part of the quarter you find the *Hospicio de Venerables Sacerdotes*, commonly called "Los Venerables". The institution was founded by Justino de Neve at the end of the 17th century. The building is baroque style and was carried out by the architect Leonardo de Figueroa. The patio, well worth a visit, is in Sevillian style. The church, which you enter through the patio has only one nave and a beautiful ceiling. It exhibits magnificent works of art, among which there can be admired paintings by Luca Valdés, representing historical episodes of the life of King Ferdinand and of the Gospel. There is also a *statue of St. Stephen*, which is believed to be by Martínez Montanes and other *paintings of St. Peter* by Pedro Roldán.

Near the Hospicio de Venerables we find the enclosure of Plaza de Doña Elvira, a square used in the 16th and 17th centuries as an open air theatre. Here the comedies by Miguel de Cervantes, the author of the famous Don Quixote, were representend by The Theatre Company of Rodrigo Ossario (1582).

SANTA MARIA LA BLANCA

On the northern side of the Santa Cruz quarter you find calle Santa María La Blanca where the ancient Sinagogue stood. Probably it stands on the site of an *earlier sinagogue*. This building was built in 1253 on the plan of an Arab mosque and was given to the Jews by King Alfonso X 'the Wise' to those who collaborated with him in his scientific works.

There is little left of the Jewish architecture and decorations because in the 14th century the synagogue was damaged by earthquakes and had to be rebuilt by King Pedro I. In 1591 it became a Catholic church and was named Paroquia de Nuestra Señora de la Nieve, and commonly called Santa María La Blanca. In the 17th century it underwent restoration work and now is Baroque churriguesc style. The high altar exhibits the painting of the *Virgen de la Nieve*, a work by Juan de Astorga. On one of the altars we find a beautiful panel representing the *Piedad*, a work by Luis de Vargas. In this church there are many paintings by Murillo and other famous painters but the French led by marshal Sault, during the war in 1808, plundered it. Later they were given back to the Spanish government but they never were taken back to Seville and they are now on display in the Royal Academy of Fine Arts of San Fernando in Madrid.

The severe architecture of the Casa Lonja which houses the precious Archive of India.

THE ARCHIVE OF INDIA

If you go along calle Ximénez Enciso you reach the cathedral. Facing the avenida de la Constitución we find the building of the Archive of India. In 1492, after the discovery of America, Seville became a trading centre for all the products which were imported by India and bought by German, French and Italian merchants. An author of the time wrote that in Seville: "You will see pearls and emeralds in sacks, just as if they were peas sold at a food market". At first the goods were sold along the streets on the steps of the cathedral but during the reign of King Philip II the merchants joined in a corporation and on 30th October 1572 they built the Casa Lonja. The house was built by the architect Juan de Herrera, the same architect of the Escorial, who was paid for this project 1,000 ducates. The building is Herrerian style and it resembles the Monastery of the Escorial. The main entrance was not, as it is now, on Avenida de la Constitución but on the Cathedral Square as you can see by a tablet on the architrave on the door. In front of the main entrance you can admire the *Cross of the Oaths* in front of which merchants swore they would deal honestly and promised they would reimburse the money if the goods were not of good quality. In the interior you still can admire the superb marble stairways and the large halls used for trading purposes.

On 25th October 1784 this building became the seat of the General Archive of India. Here all the documents of the Casa de Contratación, the Court of India and everything which was related to the Spanish colonial empire were set here. The exhibition includes the first maps and documents dating back to 1492 up to the documents which record the loss of the colonies of Cuba, Puerto Rico and the Philippines in 1898. The Archive, which displays a large collection of maps, nautical maps is not a museum. It is a very busy office which often aids the Latin American countries to solve their problems on borders considering that it preserves all the topographical maps of the colonial age.

THE TOWN HALL

After King Ferdinand had reconquested Seville, the Municipal Parliament formed by twenty-four cavalrymen and jurymen met in the Elm Courtyard, at the foot of the Giralda under the niche of the Virgen, in Plaza de la Virgen de los Reyes. It was quite clear that in the 15th century the Municipal Capitolum of Seville could not meet in such a poor courtyard, therefore the Consistorial Palace was built and the site was to be Plaza de San Francisco. In 1527 the architect Diego de Riano started the building works. The style is Renaissance. The Town Hall of Seville can be considered one of the most extraordinary monuments because of its style although its external decoration was never ended. The façade on Plaza San Francisco has many doors and large windows decorated with medalions representing mythological and historical characters. The columns are decorated with flowers and grotesque images.

On this side of the building there can be admired the famous Arquillo which connects Plaza de San Francisco to Plaza Nueva. On both sides of the Arquillo there are two nices which hold two statues: the *Statue of Hercules*, a Phoenician navigator (later venerated as a god) considered the founder of Seville and a *statue of Julius Cesar* who restored and fortified the city. Both the statues are placed here because the characters are considered fathers of the city. The facade of the Town Hall is rather modern and of little architectonical interest. In the interior of the building there is a beautiful *Capitular Hall* with a magnificent vaulted ceiling and 45 stone panels representing the Kings of Spain before Philip II. The stairways are also well worth a visit. It connects the ground floor to the first floor and is built in Gothic-Renaissance style. There are many ancient paintings in the building, mostly by famous artists, in addition to sculptures, stained glass windows and many other treasures.

The back of the Town Hall which opens onto Plaza Nueva.

THE HOUSE OF PILATE

The Palace of the Dukes Medinaceli is called Casa de Pilatos, because the Holy Week Procession started from here ending in Cruz del Campo just like Jesus Christ had left the house of Pilate to go on the Golgotha. On the façade there can be seen two tablets which mark the beginning of the Via Crucis.

The large *marble portal* was carried out in 1583 by the Italian artist Antonio María de Aprile and ordered by the first Marquis of Tarifa, Don Fadrique Enríquez de Ribera, the son of the Governor of Andalusia, don Pedro Enríquez who built the palace. The building is Renaissance style. Most of it was the work of the two brothers Aprile together with Bernardino de Bisono. All the same there are several flowered Gothic elements and Mudejar decorations. This palace is a clear example of the 16th century style. The magnificent patio is 25 meters long and 25 meters wide. In the middle there can be seen a beautiful fountain representing Gianus mounting on two dolphins. On both ends of the patio there are two beautiful statues. The former represents *Athena dressed as a warrior* whereas the latter represents *Athena in peaceful meanure*, they are both attributed to Phidia but they are most probably Roman copies. The mudejar decoration on the doors of the hall, the sumptuousness of the ancient statue representing goddesses and muses

The House of Pilate, the entrance door by Antonio María de Aprile and some images of the richly decorated building which unites various styles: Mudejar, Gothic and Renaissance.

explain why this building is considered one of the most beautiful in Seville. The building also houses an archive in which all the documents belonging to the Dukes of Alcalá and Medinaceli are preserved. Most of the members of the latter were either viceroys or embassadors at the court of the King of Naples or at the Pope's Court. The documents of this archive have an enormous historical importance. The gardens of the palace are the most beautiful and romantic gardens in the whole of Seville.

THE ANCIENT AUDIENCIA REAL

The ancient Audiencia or Casa Cuadra de Justicia is situated in Plaza de San Francisco in front of the main façade of the Town Hall. This building of noble aspect was constructed in 1597 on the site of the ancient Casa Cuadra de Justicia which dated back to the 14th century. The façade, as we see it today, was restored in 1924 by the architect Anibal González. In the interior we find a beautiful patio and a monumental flight of stairs. The building is now seat of the main offices of the Bank of San Fernando.

THE CHURCH OF SAN SALVADOR

It is near the Church of San Salvador in Plaza del Salvador. In ancient times it was the mosque of Ad-Abbas and was built around 1080 by the Arab kings. Of the mosque there survives only (after the earthquakes of the 14th century) the *Patio de los Naranjos*. The ruins of the previous demolitions have made the level of the patiorise so that the pillars have been almost completely buried and the arches open at only a meter from the ground level. Through the Patio de los Naranjos you find a door which leads into the church. On a small entrance on the wall there can be seen a beautiful marble tablet in Arab, in which, with gold letters, it is quoted that the mosque was built by King Mohamed Ben Abbad al-Motahmid al-Casim.

The temple was built in 1671 on a project by the architects Estebán García, Pedro Romero and Francisco Gómez Septier. The semispherical dome was built by Leonardo de Figueroa whereas the temple was ended in 1712 by Diego Díaz.

After the cathedral it is the largest and the most sumptuous church in Seville. Large pillars decorate its interior in addition to the solemn altar and an organ which is considered one of the best in the whole of Europe.

The altar piece by Cayetano Acosta, a follower of Churriguera, represents the *Transfiguration of Christ*. Among the many paintings of this church there can be found a painting dedicated to *St. Christopher* by Martínez Montañéz, the *Virgin of the Oath*, dating dack to the 16th century and a magnificent Jesus holding a cross on his shoulders, also known as *Jesus of the Passion* and considered the masterwork of Martínez Montañéz. The monument which the Sevillians erected in honour of Martínez Montañéz is in Plaza del Salvador on the site where the sculptor, then quite old, sat to watch the Holy Week Procession pass. On this occasion the painting was taken out of the church and the painter was said to have cried on seeing his work.

Some close ups of the Church of San Salvador with its internal patio and a suggestive image of Jesus of the Passion which is preserved in it.

THE CHURCH OF THE ANNUNCIATION

In 1565 the first house of the Society of Jesus was built. Originally it was built to house a College in which Miguel Cervantes himself studied. Later the college was moved and the building was used as the main seat by the Society of Jesus. The church was ended in 1579 and was based upon a project of the Jesuit Bustamante and was carried out by the architect Juan Ruiz. In the 18th century the Jesuits were expelled from Spain and the House passed to the University. Nowadays it is the seat of the Fine Arts Department. The building has been restored but the church is still in good condition and shows no traces of significative alterations.

The main door, overlooking calle Laraña, is decorated with a *relief of the Virgin with Child*, which according to several specialists is a work by Torrigiano; others believe it was painted by Juan Bautista Vásquez. The architecture of the temple is

Some particular views of the church of the Annunciation; the main entrance, the side altar and the tomb of Don Pedro Afán de Ribera.

variable: the ceiling is vaulted. The high altar of great artistic value has two life size statues representing *San Ignacio de Loyola and San Francisco Borja*, both works by Martínez Montañéz. The six panels which form the altar piece are by Roelas, Mohedano and El Pacheco. Two of these paintings are believed to be by Alonso Cano and represent *St. John the Baptist and St. John the Evangelist*. On both sides of the aisle there are beautiful *marble tombs* which were sculptured in Genoa by Antonio Maria Aprile. In one of these lies Don Pedro Enríquez, Governor General of Andalusia next to his wife Doña Catalina Enríquez de Ribera.

In this church, in an underground crypt, there can be admired a *pantheon* with the most famous citizens of Seville. Here there have been buried the poets Gustavo Adolfo Bécquer, Lista, Reinoso, the painter Valeriano Bécquer, the grammatist and linguist Benito Arias Montano and other famous characters like the soldiers Pedro Ponce de León and Lorenzo Suarez de Figueroa.

CALLE SIERPES

From the church of Annunciation you reach on foot calle Sierpes or calle de la Sierpe. It is one of the most historical streets in Seville and bears witness of the most important event of the past centuries.

In fact along this street, on the numerous azulejos and tablets events and famous characters are quoted. Here you find the famous Botanical Garden in which Doctor Nicolás Monardes managed to grow plants imported from India and diffused in Europe. Along this road stood the most famous tipographies of the 15th century which printed on their works "Calle Serpentina" to indicate that they were printed in calle Sierpes. Here we find the Royal Prison in which Miguel de Cervantes created his immortal work don Quixote. An azulejo on a wall quoted that this was the site of the famous playing cards tipography, owned by the Frenchman Pierre Papin. Cards soon became very popular in the picaresque novel and in the galleys which sailed the seas on their expeditions.

Along one of the foothpaths of calle Sierpes we find a small alley (calle Jovellanos) where the *chapel of St. Joseph* stands. A precious baroque style jewel. The most famous navigators, poets, authors of picaresque novels and artists of the Golden Age of Seville passed along this street.

The famous Calle Sierpes.

On the following pages, a detail of the rich decoration of the House of Pilate, the patio of the Casa de la Moneda and the statue of Mañara inside the Hospital de la Santa Caridad.

SECOND DISTRICT

Also in the second district there can be admired several monuments and works of art of great value. You enter the district through the Puerta de Jérez. You are then facing calle Maese Rodrigo along which the Casa de la Moneda is situated. This building, dating back to the 16th century was the seat of the Mint where money was minted with the gold and silver imported from the colonies and the most famous coins were minted here: doblons, ducados, centenes and the pesos fuertes better known as pesos columnarios. The North American rebels were influenced by the latter, infact the S which appeared on both sides of the coin was to become the symbol of the dollar. The bright façade of the Casa de la Moneda overlooks calle Rodríguez Jurado. In the interior there are several lanes now known by the names of San Nicolás, Habana, El Lobo, etc. Originally these were the names of the furnaces in which the metals were cast and of the laboratories in which the coins were minted. The building, which has now been restored offers only a partial idea of what it was in the past.

HOSPITAL DE LA SANTA CARIDAD

Leaving calle Santander, on the right, you encounter calle Temprado where the Hospital de la Santa Caridad is situated. It was built in the 17th century by Don Miguel de Mañara. The building consists in two different sections: the first section was used as a retreat for poor people and chronical sick elderly people, the second section is taken up by the Church of San Jorge. A scroll on the main entrance reads as follows: "Domus Pauperum, scala coeli" (House of the Poor people, a ladder to Heaven).
Don Miguel de Mañara was a knight who was condemned by the Sevillians for his superb behaviour. He later repented and dedicated his whole life to the poor. In front of the hospital there stands a small garden with a statue of Don Miguel in the act of lifting a poor man from the street (a work by the famous Susillo).
In the interior of the Hospital, open to the public

The facade of Church of San Jorge.

The internal patio of the Hospital de la Santa Caridad.

there can be admired magnificent azulejos, patios with beautiful colonnades and the rose bushes which Manara planted almost three centuries ago and which still flower.

The **Church of San Jorge** has only one nave and a cross vault. The high altar was carried out by Bernardo Simón de Pineda in Baroque style. The altar piece is a magnificent piece of art by the sculptor Pedro Roldán. It celebrates the Deposition of Christ. Below the high altar, in a cedar-wood coffin lies the body of Don Miguel de Mañara. The pulpit is richly decorated; the staircase is by Simone de Pineda and the baldachin by Pedro Roldán. Paintings by Murillo representing *Moses saved from the waters, The Feeding of the Five Thousand, St. John and St. Isabel of Ungary.* The vestibule exhibits the famous '*Novissimi*' by Valdés Real which are considered his masterworks.

The lane next to the church entrance has a very bizarre peculiarity. It is an open air cemetery: under the foothpath two famous characters of the Brotherhood of the Charity are buried.

The Triumph of Death and the altar-piece preserved inside the Church of San Jorge.

63

Some views of the Golden Tower.

GOLDEN TOWER

This tower is situated on Christopher Columbus Avenue, near the river bank. It was built around 1200 by the Moslem governor Abu Elda. The tower was given this name because it was originally decorated in golden *azulejos* and not because gold was secured in it. During the Arab domination it was used for different purposes, as a prison and sometimes as a shelter. According to tradition there lived the mistress of King Peter I, Aldonza Coronel. Later it housed the main offices of the Navy and now it is the seat of the Navy Museum which displays an interesting collection of several documents relating to the colonial Empire.

TORRE DE LA PLATA

Walking along calle Temprado towards calle Santander you catch a view of the pinnacle of the tower. The building has an octagonal plan and was built during the Arab domination. This white tower (when there were no buildings around it and all the neighbouring area was occupied by the river bank) was the starting point of the "Coracha", a section of the city wall which connected this tower to the Golden Tower.

Some images of the Plaza de Toros de la Real Maestranza: the largest arena in the whole of Spain; two of the chapels which can be found inside the complex of the Real Maestranza.

PLAZA DE TOROS DE LA REAL MAESTRANZA

The Plaza de Toros de la Real Maestranza is situated on paseo Cristobal Colón (Christopher Columbus Promenade). It is also known by the name of Flea Market Square because the bull ring was built on the site where the flea market was once held, that is where sailors and travellers exchanged pledges.

The Real Maestranza, which owns the square is a noble corporation founded by King Charles II in 1670 with the name of Real Maestranza de la Cavalería. The noblest and most influential families in Seville were members of the corporation. Its aim was to protect the chivalry and military codes. In the 18th century the corporation was authorized, by the king, to build a bull ring. The project was designed by the architect Vincente San Martín who started the building in 1761. The most noteworthy altar piece is supported by a large round-headed arch. The altar piece is decorated with Corinthian pillars and the fronton still bears traces of the royal coat of arms and other symbolic representations.

The *Chapel* is also very beautiful. It was built by the architect Anibal González and now houses the *Museum of the History of Bull Fights* with a curious display of mementos.

Teatro de la Maestranza.

Museum of Fine Arts, El Greco: the son of the Painter. ▶

Near the bull ring is situated the Casa de la Real Maestranza, the house where the knights met. The building now exhibits a rich collection of paintings by many famous artists. It has been built by the architect Anibal Gonzáles in quite recent times. On Paseo Cristobal Colón, just opposite the bull ring, there can be admired a small *statue of Carmen*; the main character of Bizet's opera, who, according to the legend, was stabbed to death by her jealous and unhappy lover, Don José, in this very place.

ST. MADELEINE'S CHURCH

Walking down calle Reyes Católicos you reach calle San Pablo, where the church of St. Madeleine is situated. The name is quite recent because it was called Church of St. Madeleine only in the 19th century when all the documents of this parish, now no longer existing, were taken here. But the original name of the church was Monastery of St. Paul and was founded by some friars of the powerful Dominican Order. Many inscriptions on the main entrance remind the visitors that the bishop of Chiapas was consacrated here, that is the famous Bartolomeo de las Casas, the author of *The Destruction of India* in which he reported the cruelty used

by the Spanish in their colonies.

The temple is what survives of one of the largest monasteries in the whole of Spain. It has a nave and two aisles and dates back to 1691, when the church was rebuilt, on the site of the medieval temple, by the architect Leonardo de Figueroa. The sculptures on the presbyterium and on the altar piece belong to the school of Pedro Roldán. They were partly carried out by La Roldana, the scultpor's daughter, and by her husband. The reliefs represent episodes of the life of the saints of the Dominican Order. The altar piece in Baroque style is a magnificent work of art. Near the door leading to the sacristy two altar pieces can be seen: the former represents the *Virgen de las Fiebres*, by Juan Bautista Vázquez (1565), the latter *St. Joaquín, St. Ann and the Holy Virgin*, a work by Ruiz Guijón. Noteworthy are also the *altar of the Virgen de la Antigua* and a large painting representing an "Auto da Fe". Many of the paintings in this church are by Luca Valdés. Among them we remember the one representing *San Christobal* and two historical paintings.

Between the 16th and the 17th centuries the Royal Monastery of St. Paul was used to celebrate several of the trials of the Inquisition. The modern church, however, built in 1691, bears no trace of this sinister past.

69

Museum of Fine Arts, Murillo: The Virgin of the Cloth.

THE MUSEUM OF FINE ARTS

Walking along calle Bailén, you come across the Museum Square where the magnificent museum building stands. Between the 16th and 17th century it housed one of the most famous monasteries of the Order of la Merced. The friars of this Order were in charge of rescuing the prisoners and hostages taken by the Berber pirates and kept in Algerian and Turkish prisons. The families of the freed prisoners were generally very generous to the Order; so it became very soon one of the richest Orders of the whole Church. Here lived, for some time, the famous Friar Gabriel Tellez, better known as Tirso de Molina, a famous comedian and representative of Spanish classicism. Among his other works he wrote *Don Juan*, which was soon translated and adapted into different languages.

The building of the monastery was carried out between 1600 and 1612 by Juan de Oviedo. The façade is decorated with a spiral column with an *image of the virgen de la Merced* and an emblem of the Order. Originally this façade was on the opposite side of the building and was moved to this side in 1940. The friars of the order lived here until the 19th century, then they were expelled and the monastery became a museum (1852). The patios, the cloister and the small yard are well worth a visit.

In the main hall of the museum, on the site of the ancient church, there can be admired the paintings by Murillo, Zurbarán, Roelas and Greco. The other halls exhibit the works of artists such as Luis de Vargas, Los Polancos, Herrera, Pacheco, Valdés Leal, Bocanegra, Castillo and the Flemish artist Martin Vos and by other modern authors like Esquivel, Sorolla, Gonzalo Bilbao and Alfonso Grosso. Several rooms are dedicated to the works of Zurbarán and Aguilar. The museum also diplays many famous statues such as *St. Jerome* by Pietro Torrigiano, a rival of Michelangelo. He is said to have hit Michelangelo in the face with a hammer when they both were working in Rome. For this violent act in a sacred temple he was forced to flee to avoid being executed. He fled to Seville and executed many of his works for the monastery of St. Jerome including this magnificent piece of sculpture. Later the Duke of Arcos commissioned a statue of the Virgin. When the duke refused to pay him asserting that the statue was "poor in quality", Torrigiano destroyed it with his hammer. He was accused of ruining and destroying a sacred image and therefore put into prison by the Inquisition. He preferred to starve to death rather than confess his crime (1528).

The Museum of Fine Arts in Seville is the second museum of Spain because of its large display of paintings and sculptures, second only to the Prado Museum in Madrid.

The *portrait of Jorge Manuel's son* by el Greco is worth seeing, in addition to the *three paintings of the Immaculate* (with Child, of the Almighty Lord and Large one), the *two busts of St. Anthony of Padua* and *the Virgin of the Cloth*, all works by Murillo. There are also works of the modern school such as *"The Last Communion of St. Ferdinand"* by Virgilio Mattoni.

Museum of Fine Arts, Murillo: San Tomás de Villanueva.
Museum of Fine Arts, Velázquez: Imposition of the planet to San Idelfonso.

On the following page, a typical Sevillian architectural work.

THIRD DISTRICT

In the third district we have divided the town center into, there can be seen the Church of San Vicente, which became a parish in the 13th century and was built on the site of an ancient Arab mosque, in the 14th century in mudejar style and later altered. The original portal was decorated with a Gothic arch, now blind, overlooking calle de San Vicente. The altar piece on the high altar is by Cristobal de Guadiz. It dates back to the end of the 17th century. In the centre there is a painting of St. Vincent attributed to Pedro Roldán. Christ Crucified, on the upper part of the altar piece is by Roque Ballduque and dates back to the 16th century. The "Christ of the Seven Words", venerated in the chapel of the Brotherhood, by Jeronimo Hernández, is also of the same period. On the left aisle there is a small chapel with a painting of the Virgen de los Remedios by Villegas Marmolejo. The chapel of the Agonizing Christ, with its magnificent altar, was believed to be a work by Pedro Roldán. This is the statue which is usually carried out during the Holy Procession. The cross in tortois e shell and silver decorations, is a masterpiece of the 18th century.

THE PARISH OF SAN LORENZO

The parish is situated not so far off, in the homonymous square. The building with a bell tower in mudejar style, built in the 15th century, is in gothic-mudejar style although it has undergone many alterations. The high altar was built by the architect Martínez Montañéz (1632) whereas the paintings are by Felipe de Rivas and Francisco Dionisio de Rivas and date back to the 17th century.

The Chapel of the Blessed Virgin exhibits a beautiful altar-piece painted by Francisco Pacheco. The painter Villegas Marmolejo is buried below one of the altars near the choir. The tomb is decorated by a statue representing a Virgin with Child by the author himself.

Notwithstanding the many precious works of art displayed in the church, the most famous painting is without doubt the Virgin of Rocamadour. The fresco has gigantic proportions: the Virgin is more than three meters high and the whole picture is more than four meters high. There are contrasting opinions on the paintings. Many critics consider it a Mozarabic painting of the 13th century, others date it back to the 14th century. However, the painting is very important in the history of art of Seville. In fact it is able to impress the visitor with its beauty and with the brightness of its colours.

The statuary group in the Chapel of St. Ann is also worth a visit. Here St. Ann is represented while she is teaching the young Virgin to read. It is a clear example of Baroque style and was carried out by the sculptor Montés de Oca.

You should also devote some time to the organ, which dates back to the 18th century, and was made by the artist Juan Calero. This piece of art is not only a magnificent instrument but it also possesses a beautiful carved sound box decorated in gold.

THE CHAPEL OF GRAN PODER

In the same square there stands the Chapel or Temple of Our Holy and Almighty Lord, which was built by the architects Antonio Delgado Roig and Antonio Balbontín Orta around 1960.

The image of Our Almighty Lord is situated in a niche (which can be visited) on the high altar. It is a masterpiece of the religious Sevillian imagination. The image was painted by the famous Juan de Mesa at the beginning of the 17th century. The painting represents Christ in the act of holding the cross on his shoulder and showing on his body the marks of the tortures he has suffered; these details are represented in a realistic style.

THE TOWER OF DON FADRIQUE

From the compás of St. Clara you pass through a beautiful wrought iron gate and enter another patio in which the Don Fadrique tower stands. Half of the tower is Romanic style whereas the upper part is Gothic style. It is a clear example of transition between two different architectonical styles. It was built by the Infante Don Fadrique, the son of Ferdinand. After he was murdered by his brother, Alfonso X 'the Wise', all his villa and his gardens were given to the Franciscan Order so that the Convent of St. Clara could be built. The tower was left to guard the Town Hall (Ayuntamiento), to which it still belongs. The patio in front of the Tower is used as an open air museum because it displays important archeological remains belonging to the city.

THE CONVENT OF ST. CLARA

Proceeding along calle Santa Clara you reach the convent which bears the same name. Its façade has much in common with the neighbouring buildings; it possesses a 18th century *azulejo* representing St. Clara with an ostensorium in her hand. From here you enter a *compás* (atrium), that is the external patio which is not directly connected to the main building. In the middle of the *compás* there stands a precious fountain with orange trees. The portico at the far end of this patio leads to the church portal. Curiously enough in front of the main entrance there stands a tomb with an inscription which informs the visitor that it is the burial place of a noblewoman. She was buried on the threshold of the convent because her daughters were enclosed nuns of the convent and therefore could not be buried in the convent itself. Her name was Doña Juana Salgado and she died in 1614.

The church, in Gothic-mudejar style, dates back to he 14th century, whereas its socle is decorated with Sevillian *azulejos*. The high altar, by Martínez Montañés, and all its paintings were done between 1612 and 1626. The two altar pieces on the right wall are also by Montañés and the paintings representing, respectively St. John the Baptist and St. Roccus, are by Ocampo and Esturmio. The Convent also displays other sacred objects, among which a Renaissance pyx dating back to the 16th century.

On the previous pages the 'Jesus de las Penas' preserved in the Church of San Vicente and the 'Jesus del Gran Poder', preserved in the Chapel of Gran Poder.

Some decorative details of the facades of the Convents of St. Clara and St. Clements.

The main entrance of the church of the Convent of St. Clements.

THE CONVENT OF ST. CLEMENT

The Monastery of St. Clement is situated in calle St. Clara. This monastery, according to tradition was the summer palace of the Moorish king, but it has undergone so many alterations that there are no traces of the ancient building. You enter the monastery through a façade, dating back to the 17th century, and through a compass or external patio which leads to the church.

The *high altar* is by Felipe de Ribas (1640). It is decorated with paintings representing St. Clement, St. Bernard and St. Benito, patrons of the Cistercian Order. There are frescoes by Juan Valdés Leal, one of these illustrates an historical event: the *arrival of St. Ferdinend in Seville*.

The altar piece representing the *Virgin of the Kings*, which dates back to the reign of St. Ferdinand (1248) is part of the so-called "ferdinandeian series" of which the Virgin in the Cathedral is part too. The sepulchral *tomb of queen Mary of Portugal*, the wife of Alfonso XI and mother of Pedro I is well worth a visit. It is sumptuously decorated with *azulejos* and always covered with a red drape and a crown.

CALLE CALATRAVA

If you walk round St. Clement's Monastery you reach calle Calatrava which takes its name from the Monastery of the military Order of Calatrava. Now the Monastery is called Parish of Nuestra Señora de Belén. The building bears traces of the ancient military Order and in particular there still survive two stone coat of arms on the upper part of the wall. The legend says that Don Juan abducted a young nun, Doña Inés de Ullos from this very same monastery.

Farther along the street, on the right, we find another chapel or hermitage, dedicated to Our Lady of Mount Carmel, dating back to the 17th century. The historical documents report that the chapel was built by the Marquises of Tarifa for the soul of their son, Don Pedro Ribera (the Younger), who died here. The square was then called Plaza de la Cruz del Rodeo and the young marquis was stabbed to death by the family of a young woman he had abducted. It seems this episode influenced the legend of the *Stone Guest* by adding to the original plot the abduction of a young woman.

FOURTH DISTRICT

The last district we shall visit starts off from the Promenade de la Alameda de Hércules.

Originally there could be found the bed of the river Guadalquivir before King Leovigildus changed its course in the 7th century. There still exists a small lake which used to fill with water in winter and infest the city with mosquitoes in summer. For this reason, the Intendant Don Francisco de Zapata y Cisneros, Count of Barajas, had the marsh drained in the 16th century and poplars planted. That is why the site was called Promenade de la Alameda (alameda=poplar). Here were built three artistical fountains and two gigantic Roman columns, which originally stood in calle Marmoles and were remains of an ancient Roman temple, were later brought here to decorate the promenade. A marble tablet, at the foot of one of the columns states that their transportation was "ar-duous and resembled one of the labours of Hercules". Two statues were placed on the top of the columns. They represent Hercules and Julius Cesar and were sculptured by Diego de Pesquera, who depicted the traits of Charles I in the face of Hercules and Philip II in the statue of Cesar.

The Promenade of Alameda soon became, from the moment it was built (1574) one of the most elegant sites in the whole of Europe. In the 18th century the northern part was completed by the addition of two more columns; they are decorated with a lion and coat of alms of the Royal Army and the Town Hall of Seville. The Promenade was deteriorated in the 19th century and soon became a meeting place for vagrants and criminals. So the elegant and noble families preferred Paseo de las Delicias and the Salón de Cristina, at the opposite side of the city.

◄ A suggestive image of the Virgen de la Macarena.

Some views of the Roman columns and of one of the fountains which can be admired along the Promenade of Alameda de Hércules.

The 18th century Puerta de la Macarena.

THE BASILICA OF THE MACARENA

If you walk along calle Feria and turn right into calle Resolana you come to the Basilica de la Macarena, a modern church built by the architect Gómez Millán in 1949, on behalf of the Brotherhood del Señor de la Sentencia and for the Virgen de la Esperancia Macarena, whose temple was destroyed by the revolutionaries in 1936.

The façade of the basilica is regionalistic Andalusian style whereas the interior is neo-baroque style. A tablet on the façade states that the church has been officially named basilica.

A shrine with the image of the Virgen Macarena stands on the high altar. The shrine is visibile to the public and its walls were chased by the famous goldsmith Fernando Marmolejo. The shrine is a masterpiece of goldsmithery.

The *image of the Virgen de la Esperancia Macarena* is one of the most famous sculptures in Seville. It dates back to the Baroque period and it is believed to be the work of the famous sculptor Luisa Roldán de Mena, known as La Roldana, the only woman who managed to become the official sculptor of the Spanish Court. Many of her works, dating back to the 17th century, can still be admired in the Royal Palace in Madrid.

The church also celebrates the *Señora de la Sentencia*, a work by the sculptor Morale Nieto (1654).

At the rear of the church, on the left, there can be visited a chapel with the sepulchre of General Queipo de LLana, one of the protagonists of the Civil War which took place in 1936-1939.

On the left wall a door leads to the *Museum of the Order de la Macarena*. Here is situated the famous group representing *the Judgement of Christ* and other characters (including a Roman figure), a work by Antonio Castillo Lastrucci. The museum displays a *collection of embroidery work* among which the most beautiful examples of this art can be seen. There are also many examples of silversmithery which give an idea of the importance attributed to religious processions in Seville.

Two images of the Group of the Judgement of Christ preserved in the Museum of the Order of the Macarena.

On the following pages, two images of the Virgen de la Macarena.

Two close ups of the Wall of the 'Macarena'.

THE WALL OF THE MACARENA

Beside the Basilica stands the *Arch of the Macarena*, an ancient door of the city wall. From it we can admire a vast stretch of this wall with its towers, retaining wall, buttress and moat. This complex of fortifications was the most important in Spain, to such a point that King Alfonso X "the Wise" affirmed that many big cities could be considered well protected only if surrounded by a wall and buttress.

The wall is Roman, dating back to Augustan Age, although it was rebuilt in the Visigothic reign following destruction by Vandals, in the Arab period, so that at present, it is extensively rebuilt compared with its original Roman state. However it is a curious example of military architecture which has resisted throughout the centuries.

THE TOWERS OF ST. MARK AND ST. MARINA

Passing under the arch of the 'Macarena' we enter Calle San Luis. Going along this street one can admire on the left footpath two parish churches close to each other. One is St. Marina's and the other St. Mark's. The towers of the churches are worth mentioning. Both have been made from towers in splendid Moslem style even though there exists a certain difference of opinion among those critics who consider them 12th century works of the Almohade period and others who consider them Mudejar works of art which were already built in Christian times and precisely in the 14th century. However it may be we are dealing with two magnificent towers with their exquisite filigree work, of the same standard as the brick decoration work, they are sisters of the Giralda.

THE CHURCH OF ST. LOUIS

In this same calle, on the right hand footpath is situated Saint Louis' church, which is part of an ancient novitiate of the Society of Jesus.

The façade is attributed to Leonardo de Figueroa, the greatest architect of the end of the 17th century, however it appears that the Society of Jesus compelled him to follow the outline of another architect, Romero, with warlike tendencies who conditioned the style of the temple changing it into a frenetic baroque style. In any case, the façade of the church is one of the finest works of its time. In fact in it can be found boldly combined stone and brick, a superb sculptural ornament with figures of three archangels and two bell towers which rise at the sides of the porch and frame the façade.

The inside is very rich: the high altar occupies the centre, a *lifesize portrait of St. Louis* done by Zurbarán. The remaining part of the altar-piece is made up of thirty smaller paintings, some of which are also by Zurbarán. There accompany the high altar various other altars dedicated to the most important Jesuit saints: San Ignacio de Loyola, San Francisco de Borja, San Luis Gonzaga, San Stanislao de Kotska, St. John, San Francisco Regis and San Francisco Javier. All the images are done by the sculptor Duque Cornejo. The paintings of these altars are the work of Domingo Martínez (1750).

The towers of St. Mark and St. Marina.

ALL SAINTS' TOWER

Proceeding toward calle Perís Mencheta you reach calle de la Feria, where the Church of All Saints is situated. The façade of the church is Gothic style like many of the other churches which were rebuilt by Pedro I in the 14th century. The bell tower was believed to have been built during the Arab domination: Alejandro Guichot thought it dated back to the Almohade period, Tubinus and Belmonte, together with Gestoso believed it dated back to the same period. Nowadays most critics consider it a *mudejar* building erected at the beginning of the 15th century. The tower, however, is in brickwork and has the same type of decorations as the Giralda or very similar to it.

The ancient altar pieces disappeared together with all the paintings and pictures, painted by great artists from the 15th to the 18th centuries. In 1936 they were still on display in the church when the building was burnt by the revolutionaries. For this reason the interior of the church does not prove to be very interesting.

THE PALACE DE LAS DUEÑAS

The Palace de las Dueñas, the Sevillian residence of the Dukes of Alba can be found in the homonymous calle. This dwelling was built in the 15th century for Pineda family, who, in 1438 were obliged to sell it to pay ransom for their son Don Juan, who had been imprisoned by the Moors in the Granada war. First it passed into the hands of doña Catalina Ribera and subsequently to the Dukes of Alba

The building is *Mudejar* style with splendid stucco-work patios. Moresque arches and fillets of *azulejos* alternating with ornamentations, of Moslem taste, of Gothic style structures and ornate Gothic style which characterize galleries and halls.

In the history of this building there stands out a noteworthy event, the fact that the Empress of France, Eugenia de Montijo, widow of Emperor Napoleon III had resided here in the last years of her life and that in this same palace was born the poet Antonio Machado, the son of the administrator.

The bell tower of All Saints'Church, commonly known as the Tower of Omnium Sanctorum, and a detail of the facade of the Palace de las Dueñas.

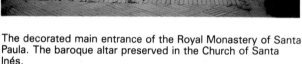

The decorated main entrance of the Royal Monastery of Santa Paula. The baroque altar preserved in the Church of Santa Inés.

THE ROYAL MONASTERY OF SANTA PAULA

The entrance to this royal monastery of the nuns of the Hieronymian Order opens onto calle Santa Paula by way of a "compás" or outer patio, where it is possible to admire the façade of the church, a work of excellent quality in which collaborated the sculptor Pedro Millán, who carried out the angels and medallions and the Italian ceramist Nicola Pisano who took care of the work of azulejos. The complex is of surprising beauty and dates back to the last years of the dominion of the Christian Monarchs (1500 approx.). The church is imposing and very rich, as rich as the order of the Hieronymites, which was always protected by the Kings of Spain. Among the sculptors stands out the one of *Santa Paula*, on the high altar, attributed to Ocampo (16th century) and the *image of St. John the Baptist* on the homonymous altar, the work of Martinez Montañés (17th century). Also work of Montañés is *St. John the Evangelist* on the opposite altar. Interesting too are the sepulchres in azulejos of the Marquises of Montemayor (16th century).

The monastery possesses a museum with numerous pictorial works, sculptures and gold-work.

THE CONVENT OF SANTA INES

In calle Doña María Coronel stands the convent of Santa Inés, founded in the 15th century by Doña Maria Coronel, a heroine of castity, who deliberately disfigured her face by pouring boiling oil over it so as not to be the mistress of King Pedro I. The corpse of this virtuous noble woman is shown to the public every year on her saint's day and it is still possible to see the terrile scars on her face.

The church is in *Mudejar* style, although it has been altered to a great extent in the 17th century. The *high altar-piece* is Baroque, the work of the brothers Francisco and Fernando de Medinilla (18th century) who were inspired by the school of Narciso Tomé and Churriguera.

The *image of Santa Inés* is by Francisco de Ocampo (17th century). There are also other images by various artists, all very worthy of praise. There are also paintings, among which an altar-piece with Flemish panels. According to the legend written by Gustavo Adolfo Bécquer, the organ of this church played during a Christmas Mass without anybody touching it, animated by the spirit of the organist Maese Pérez, who had died without being able to complete the orchestration.

The facade of the Church of St. Catherine, its portal in Mudejar style and the crucifix with the Christ of the Confraternity of Exaltation.

The Chapel of the Puerta de Jérez.

THE CHURCH OF ST. CATHERINE

Going down calle Almirante Apodaca, on the left hand side is situated the church of St. Catherine, a church which has two superimposed portails: one in stone, which came from the church of Santa Lucia and was brought here, and the original portail in mudejar style like the interior of the church which has a very rich carved ceiling. The crossing is Gothic style. The *sacristy* is Baroque, a work by Leonardo de Figueroa. Among its images is to be mentioned the *Virgen del Carmine*, the work of Gutierrez Cano (19th century) and the *Crucifixion* by García de la Vega (17th century), but above all the *Christ of the Confraternity of Exaltation*, a work by Pedro Roldán. They are part of a sculptural group of the Confraternity which is carried in the Holy Week Procession: the two thieves crucified beside Jesus and the four angels of the Passion at the corners of the group are all works of Roldana. At the foot of the church is the altar of Santa Lucia, the patron of the seamstresses and the blind, with an image of the 17th century. Cervantes, in his intermezzo, entitled *Los Mirones*, refers to this church of St. Catherine, near whose rear facade, between the end of the 16th century and the beginning of the 17th, the blind beggars gathered to sing religious romances.

THE CHAPEL OF PUERTA DE JEREZ

If we are mentioning a small chapel, built in the square of Puerta de Jérez, it is because it belongs to the ancient University of Santa María de Jesús. The building, in ornate Gothic style, has a facade in bricks and granite. Inside it is aisleless; the presbytery is preceded by a delightful ornate Gothic arch followed by a cross vault. The altar-piece, with homonymous tables of the 16th century, is an example of transition style between Gothic and Renaissance. The table in the centre represents the *Virgin of Antigua* and before her, kneeling Maese Rodrigo de Santaella in the act of offering her the miniature of the university building, which was founded by him. This is a work of the beginning of the 16th century carried out by the great master Alejo Fernández. The socle in *azulejos* and the tiled ceiling in *mudejar* style are just as worthy of mention.

The chapel is the only trace of the original Hispanic University, which was once one of the most ancient in Europe.

There are many more churches and convents in Seville. In the historical centre that we have just passed through there are twenty-four parishes and over twenty convents. We have chosen the most interesting as a significant example of the artistic treasures of the city.

ART OUTSIDE THE CITY WALL

Outside the ancient city wall can be found some artistic monuments which are just as interesting and worth visiting also because some of them are built just few metres from those which have already been visited.

THE HOSPITAL DE LAS CINCO LLAGAS

Opposite the walls of the Macarena stands the Hospital de las Cinco Llagas (the Hospital of the Five Sores) founded in virtue of a papal bill issued by Pope Alexander VI who authorized doña Catalina Ribeira to personally set up and finance a hospital in Seville. Some years later the temporary building in Calle Santiago was transferred definitely to this place by will of the first Marquis of Tarifa, Don Fabrique Enríquez de Ribera, Doña Catalina's son who charged Martín Gainza to build it. The face is instead attributed to Asensio de Maeda. The very large

building is gifted with marvellous patios and galleries. The church in the form of a Latin cross with a vaulted ceiling is in sobre neoclassical style. Now the building – which has no longer been a hospital for some years has been rebuilt to make space for the Autonomous Government of Andalusia.

THE HOSPITAL OF ST. LAZARUS

Half a kilometre away, on the right of the hospital of Las Cinco Llagas, stands the hospital of St. Lazarus, an ancient Arab palace formerly the residence of the Vizir. This building through phonetical changes ended up by being called in the following centuries "Cortijo de Gausín". It was assigned to give hospitality to lepers and was transformed into a hospital by King St. Ferdinand in 1250. It benefited by royal protection until the 19th century when leprosy died out and was turned into a charitable institution. The

◀ The facade of the Hospital de las Cinco Llagas, a work by Asensio de Maeda.

The Hospital of St. Lazarus.

The Hospital of St. Lazarus: a 17th century azulejo.

building still has a facade in bricks of the 16th century with a curious *azulejo* decoration of the 17th century. The church of the Hospital of St. Lazarus has a high altar, an altar piece in Baroque style (dating back to the 18th century), whose paintings, representing *scenes of the life of Christ* are by Villegas Marmolejo (16th century). The altar piece has been officially declared cultural property of the state. At the side of the building on the facade facing Seville, there is the small *Tower del Gausín*, in Arab style, most probably dating back to the 11th century.

THE CEMETERY OF ST. FERDINAND

A little farther on from St. Lazarus is situated the Cemetery of St. Ferdinand or municipal cemetery of Seville, built in the middle of the 19th century and inaugurated in January 1853. What is particular about this cemetery is that it looks more like a garden than a burial ground and is also a rich museum of sculpture and a historical archive of the city.
We draw your attention among the other mausoleums of bull fighters to the *tombs of Joselito, Rafael el Gallo and of Ignacio Sánchez Mejiás*, made

of a magnificent monument in bronze, the superlative work of the sculptor Mariano Benlliure and on which is represented life-size, a group of gypsies who are holding the lifeless body of Joselito on their shoulders. Beside this mausoleum we can find the *tomb of the bull fighter Paquirri*, Victor Ochoa's work, this too in bronze, representing the bull fighter in the act of making a "pase" (a movement of the cape by the matador) to guide the bull's final attack.
A short distance away we can find the *tomb of the bull fighter El Espartero*; he too died at a tender age. This fact is symbolized by the broken column.
In the middle of the cemetery stands the *Cristo de los Mieles*, the work of Antonio Susillo who is buried at its foot. In the same small square is *Christ crucified*, the work in marble of Delgado Brackembury.
In the central path, on the right, can be found the *tomb of the flamenco dancer Pedro Vega*, represented in the sculpture in flamenco costume. Another dancer's tomb stands along the last of the paths which make up the cemetery: this is the *sepulchre of Farruquito*, who died at the age of eighteen; his statue, on the eastern side, represents him interpreting his last flamenco.
It's a remarkable cemetery, which is well worth a visit for its artistic value.

THE CONVENT OF THE CAPUCHINS

Going from the Basilica of the 'Macarena' towards the right, not far away we come to the Convent of the Capuchins founded in 1627. It offers more historical testimonies than artistic values. Here for several years worked Bartolomé Esteban Murillo, who carried out many of his most famous paintings, such as *"Christ tearing off his arm from the Cross to embrace St. Francis"*, *"The Virgin of the Altar-Cloth"*, *"St. Antony of Padua with Child Jesus"*, *"St. Felicius of Cantalicio"*, *"St. Joseph"* and *"St Thomas of Villanueva who is giving alms to the poor"*. All these paintings can now be admired in the Provincial Museum of Fine Arts, in the Museum Square.

Of what is now preserved inside the Convent of the Capuchins it is worth mentioning two tablets in 15th century style by Virgilio Mattoni, representing *Santa Isabel and San Bonaventura*, as well as the extraordinary *altar of the Divine Shepherdess*, a cross between an altar piece and a theatrical scene-painting.

The Tower of St. Lazarus, and the mausoleum of Joselito in the Cemetery of St. Ferdinand.

On the next page some tombs of famous personages buried in the Cemetery of St. Ferdinand.
Above the tomb of the bull-fighter Paquirri and of the flamenco-dancer Pedro Vega, the so called «tumbas de colore».

93

THE CHURCH OF THE HOLY TRINITY

Still a little farther ahead, on the same foothpath, is situated the church of the ancient Trinity Convent, now a Salesian college. A building of huge proportions, the church dates back to the 17th century although it was built on the foundations of an earlier church, going back to the 12th century and this in its turn had been built on some Roman ruins. Inside there still exist some underground passages which, according to tradition, were the Roman praetorium prisons, where Santa Giusta and Santa Rufina, martyrs during the persecution of Diocletian and now patrons of the city, were imprisoned.
The altars do not offer works of exceptional interest, except for the high altar, a work in marble of the 19th century, with three paintings by the artist Cabral Bejaro (1814) representing the *Holy Trinity, St. John of Mata and St. Felix of Valois*. Among the aisle chapels of the Gospel an image of *St. Joseph* of the school of Martínez Montañés catches one's eye. The *image of the Virgin of Hope*, of the Brotherhood of the Sacred Providence, venerated in this church, a sculpture by the famous Juan de Astorga, dating back to 1820, is carried out in the procession every year during Holy Week.

THE CHURCH OF SAN BENITO

At the beginning of the calle Luis Montoto, on the left pavement, we can find the church of San Benito, architecturally one of the most beautiful churches in Seville. It is the work of the architect Juan de Oviedo, who carried it out at the beginning of the 17th century. The ogival arches held up by coupled columns, give this church an elegant and original characteristic, however much of it had to undergo fires and floods. On the high altar there are *valuable images* of the Virgin of Valvanera, St. Francis, Santa Clara, St. Bernard and St. Ferdinand, all belonging to the 17th century as well as the painting of San Benito placed in the centre, high up on the altar, dating back, probably, to the 16th century. There are also some beautiful 18th century paintings.
On the altars of the Brotherhood, which has its see in this church, their valuable titular images are venerated: the *Christ of the Most Precious Blood*, by Francisco Buiza, the *Christ of the Presentation*, by Antonio Castillo Lastrucci, both belonging to this century, and the *Virgin of the Incarnation* by an anonymous 17th century artist.

A view of the rich decoration in the interior of the Church of the Holy Trinity.

Church of San Benito: a detail of the central nave.

On the following pages a beautiful image of the Christ of the Confraternity, the Cruz del Campo (Cross of the Field) and the Royal Tobacco Factory, seat of the Hispalense University.

CRUZ DEL CAMPO

At the end of the same calle Luis Montoto, half hidden among the buildings that have grown up around, we can find the Cruz del Campo: a 15th century cross, made in 1482 by the Intendant of Seville, Don Diego de Merlo. It is made up of a pavilion in Gothic-mudejar style bricks placed on a platform with steps. Four pillars with strong counterforts support a dome in bricks of octagonal design. Below this tabernacle there is a marble column which supports a cross on which are carved the images of Jesus Christ and the Virgin.

This cross was used as the final Station of the way of the Cross in the procession, as we have already mentioned in the previous pages. It started off at the Casa de Pilatos on Good Friday.

THE ROYAL TOBACCO FACTORY

Built in Calle San Fernando, the Royal Tobacco Factory is now used as the seat of the Hispalense University for which the building has been adapted in the middle of this century. We owe the construction of this remarkable building to the initiative of King Fernando VI (the initial project belonged to the military engineer Ignacio Sala) even if the construction was directed by Johann Van dem Berg, to whom we also owe the main face and the entrance portal. It was completed by the architects Catalán and Bengoechea.

Here we are dealing with the largest complex in the whole of Spain, exceeded only by the Escorial, built in the same period. It measures 177 metres by 98. Inside there are 44 patios. Due to the importance of tobacco which constituted one of the main sources of income in industry at a time when Spain was the only European country to produce this plant. A fact that authorized the monopoly and the consequent control of prices, and they adopted very strict measures in order to avoid thefts, so much so that the factory building was fortified with sentry boxes for the sentinels and the entrance was equipped with a draw bridge. Of all this now there remains 300 metres of ditch and numerous sentry-boxes on the face overlooking the Park of María Luisa.

The impressiveness of the interior is accompanied by an exceptional architectural level, enriched by the use of precious materials, by sumptuous staircases and by a great variety of fountains in the patios. The porch is superb, decorated by busts of Columbus and Cortés and by the embellished coat of arms and on the top of the fronton, by a statue of Glory in the act of blowing a trumpet and by groups of vases of lilies. In front of the main entrance there used to be a guard provided by the Dragoon Regiment. It is just in this place, according to the legend, that Carmen, a cigar-maker in this factory, and Don José who was a sergeant of the Dragoon Guard fell in love, a love that was used as the starting point for the story of the opera Carmen.

The Park of María Luisa with its monument to the poet, a work by the Sevillian sculptor Coullat Valera.

THE PARK OF MARIA LUISA

Beside the Royal Tobacco Factory, after crossing the Glorieta del Cid, we enter the park of María Luisa. This is a garden which is two kilometers long and nearly one kilometre wide. It was designed at the beginning of the 20th century from the garden of the Palace of San Telmo, which was donated by the Infante María Luisa to be used as a public park. The gardens of Mariana and other small holdings were added until the present day size was reached. We owe the structure of the Park to the famous architect of gardens Leforestier.

Inside the Park were set up the pavilions for the Hispo-American Fair of 1929 and they are grouped in several complexes.

Plaza de España is made up from the complex of buildings used as the office for the 1929 Fair. They form a compact architectural unity in a semicircular design with two towers, at the north and south end. The majestic complex is the work of the architect Aníbal González who was able to unite a delightful harmony of marble, brick. and Sevillian azulejos, obtaining a perfect overall effect. The buildings are at present occupied by public offices and by the General Office of the regional Army. In front of the hemicycle of the buildings runs a gallery which passes into another gallery decorated by panels of *azulejos*, one for every province of the country of Spain; which bear frontal allegorical paintings in ceramics regarding the history of the respective province. In front, crossed by various bridges decorated with *azulejos* and polychrome ceramics runs a canal along which small boats can sail.

Plaza de America is made up of several palaces which are different in architecture. There is the *Royal Pavilion* in flamboyant Gothic style. The *Archeological Museum*, in Renaissance style and the *Mudejar Pavilion*, in its relative style, all three are carried out by the same Aníbal González. The Mudejar Pavilion houses the *Museum of Popular Arts.*

On this and the following pages some views of Plaza de España and its magnificent ceramic-panelled benches: an allegory of the fifty-eight provinces of Spain.

The facade of the Archaeological Museum.

Some Iberian antiquities belonging to the Treasure of Carambolo.

Archaeological Museum: two famous ancient statues: ▶
the Venus of Italica and the great torso of Diana.

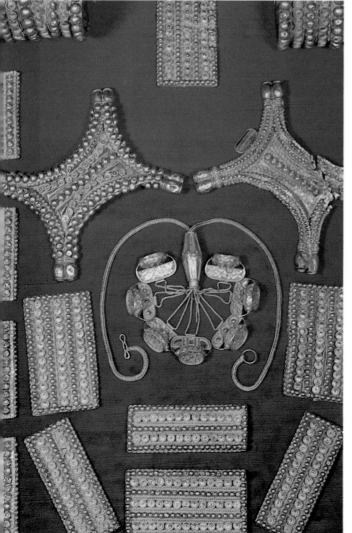

THE ARCHAEOLOGICAL MUSEUM

Possesses one of the richest collections of Roman statues and mosaics in the whole of Spain. There stand out the *statue of Ermes* (2nd century approx.), the *statue of Trajan*, the *bust of Adrian* and the *great torso of Diana* which, because of its perfection, is considered by some to be a Greek work, but it is generally considered a Roman production.
There are also rooms which are very rich in Iberian antiquity, including the famous *treasure of Carambolo*.

Two views of the Museum of Arts and Popular Customs.

OTHER BUILDINGS OF THE IBERIAN-AMERICAN FAIR

In the Park of María Luisa remain many buildings that at the time of the Fair in 1929 were used as pavilions, such as the *Lope de Vega Theatre* and the *Fair Casino*. Also the pavilions which were built for the various exhibiting countries still remain, in particular those of Chile, Peru, Mexico, Colombia and Guatemala constructed in the architectural style of the country represented.

Museum of Arts and Popular Customs. It contains a great variety of collections, among which crochet work, ceramics and china, court costumes, tools, farming implements and objects used for work regarding cattle raising and tillage. We can find displayed also furnished habitations belonging to different periods as well as complete artisan shops. The collection of traditional Andalusian costumes is very interesting.

THE PALACE OF SAN TELMO

Leaving the Park of María Luisa again in the direction of the historical centre, after crossing the Paseo de las Delicias, we come across the Palace of San Telmo, built for the Seminary College of Marcantes and also called the Pilots' School of the Route of the Indies (Pilotas de la Carrera de Indias). It was carried out in 1682 on the project of Leonardo de Figueroa and his son Matias.

It is Baroque style, characterized by a redundant decoration inside the halls, galleries and patios. The face has a sculpture of San Telmo, the patron of seamen in the act of holding a boat in his hand. When the School was closed down in 1847, the palace was purchased two years later by Anthony of Orleans, the Duke of Montpensier, who made it his residence. Here was born little Mercedes who married Alfonso XII and was an unfortunate Queen of Spain.

The building was enriched by a row of *statues* placed on a balustrade of the terrace on the north side. These life-size statues overlooking the street below, represent personages of the history of Seville among whom Bartholemew de las Casas, Murillo, Vélazquez, Daoiz and others who distinguished themselves in arms, letters and arts. They are all works of Antonio Susillo.

The palace used to have large gardens that the infanta María Luisa donated to the city and even today they make up the Park of María Luisa. The Infanta gave up the building to the church for it to house the Seminary. At present the Autonomous Government of Andalusia has been transferred there and therefore it has been turned into the Presidential Palace.

THE DISTRICT OF LOS REMEDIOS

Crossing the bridge of San Telmo, on the other bank of Guadalquivir, we come to the district of Los Remedios, which is modern and without any artistic interest. However in the Plaza de Cuba, which is situated in correspondence with the beginning of the bridge there is the small building of the *ancient convent of Nuestra Señora de los Remedios*, which at present has been turned into offices for EXPO-92. On the east side of this building, overlooking the river it is possible to see a big memorial tablet which recalls that here disembarked, together with the sailors of the Victoria, Juan Sebastian Elcano, the first seaman to carry out a periplus of the world.

The Palace of San Telmo — the residence of the Dukes of Montpensier — a detail of the facade.

THE DISTRICT OF TRIANA

From the same Plaza de Cuba, going northwards, we enter the District of Triana, which in Roman times was the centre of the production of terracotta pottery, jugs and amphoras used for the exportation of corn and oil from Seville to Rome. In this distirct there worked as potters two sisters Giusta and Rufina, Holy martyrs and patrons of Seville.

On the river bank facing the Golden Tower there used to be a fortress whose name the corresponding street bears. In the centre of the district we can find *St. Anna's church*, built by King Alfonso X 'the Wise' as thanksgiving after being restored to health after an acute glaucoma.

The church is the first building to have been built between the Reconquest and 1280, in Romanesque Mudejar style. Romanesque too are the lions' heads which make up the ornamentation of the upper part, while the rest was modified in the baroque period. The interior, a rectangular design with apses and a vaulted roof solves the problem of the pressure of the central aisle on the two sides relieving the weight on the external buttresses, a technical solution planned by the Romanesque architects of Poitou who reached Spain, according to Hernández Díaz and Sancho Corbacho through the Cistercian Order. The bell tower is an example of early Mudejar with blank windows and multifoiled arches.

For its proportions and because it has always been the main church in this district, it is traditionally called the Cathedral of Triana and, in one way, it benefitted from priviledges similar to those of a cathedral.

The high altar is Renaissance style although the two images that occupy the central niche and that represent St. Ann and the Virgin are 12th century works, while the Child whom the Virgin is holding in her arms appears to be a later work. The altar piece is completed by fifteen paintings on a tablet representing *episodes of the life of St. Joaquín, St. Ann and the Virgin Mary*, works of the artists Andrés Ramírez, Pedro Jiménez and Master Pedro de Campaña (1564). It is well worth noticing the *altar of St. Theresa of Avila* with the clothed saint accompanied by five paintings representing saints of the 16th century Flemish school. In the aisle of the Epistle there can be found other paintings, representing the *Adoration of the Magi, St. Giusta and St. Rufina* and other saints, all works of Alejo Fernández. There is also an *altar of the Divine Shepherdess*, with images by Gabriel Astorga.

The private chapels all over the church are very interesting. They were financed by sea captains and contain family tombs, some of which of certain value. Also Nicola Pisano's ceramic decorations are important.

Even without any other reasons the richness of the church alone would be sufficient for the church to deserve the name of Cathedral of Triana.

The Church of St. Anna with its Virgin and Child.

Isabella II Bridge also known as the Bridge of Triana and a characteristic view of the district.

THE BRIDGE OF TRIANA

Not far from here there is the famous bridge of Triana, whose real name is Isabella II Bridge. It crosses the Guadalquivir and is built in the same place where, in the middle ages, there was the boat bridge built by the Almohads. This bridge is one of the first iron bridges in Spain and was built in 1846 by the Belgian engineers. Steinacher and Rouhault who got inspiration from the Carrousel bridge in Paris.

CALLEJON DE LA INQUISICION

Opposite Isabella II bridge is situated Plaza del Altoxano, where the Market of Triana has its building and it occupies the spot of the ancient castle of St. George where, for three centuries there was the Prison of the Inquisition, a gloomy building full a sinister memories which was pulled down following the suppression of the Tribunal of the Holy Inquisition. However, at the beginning of Calle Castilla there remain some traces right here in Callejón de la Inquisición (Inquisition Lane) which from the calle crosses the buildings as far as the river.

The Chapel of Patronage and the Callejón de la Inquisición.

The Christ Crucified, popularly called «El ►
Cachorro» and the Virgin of the Patronage, preserved in
the homonymous chapel.

THE CHAPEL OF PATRONAGE

Along Calle Castilla on the right we come to the church of Hope in which the Virgin of the Confraternity of Hope is venerated. It is the building of the ancient Almonas de Jabón, the Duke of Alcala's soap manufacturers, it has now been transformed into a civil residence. At the end of the street there is the Chapel of Patronage. Inside it is possible to admire the *image of Christ on the Cross*, a work by Ruiz Gijón (1682). This Christ crucified is popularly called "El cachorro" (the Pup), as according to tradition, the artist got his inspiration from the agonizing face of a gypsy known as El Cachorro who had been stabbed. This Christ on the Cross, according to some authors is the work of the greatest realism of Sevillian baroque. The Virgin of the Patronage, the same of the homonymous confraternity was also an 18th century work but it was destroyed in 1973 when an accidental fire broke out. In just one month the young sculptor Luis Alvárez Duarte carved another image of the Virgin for the Holy Week procession.

THE UNIVERSAL EXHIBITION OF 1992 FAIR

On 12th October 1986 His Majesty Juan Carlos I, the King of Spain, in a message directed to all the peoples of the world, solemnly announced that in 1992 there would be held a universal Exhibition to commemorate the Discovery of America and to which all nations were invited. The work on this Exhibition began straight away, classified by the International Committee of Festivities and Shows with the name of top level Universal Exhibition and for which the centre was chosen on the island of Cartuja, on the other bank of the Guadalquivir, opposite the historical centre of the city. A Professor holding a Chair in law at the Hispalense University, Manuel Olirencia was appointed Commissioner responsible for the realization of the Exhibition. So they began to adapt the island of Cartuja (Certosa Island) delimited by two branches of the river, the old course and the building of the Certosa, as well as working to improve the Sevillian road network; the deviation of railway lines and the building of a new station at Saint Justa; the adaption of the San Pablo airport with the building of a new terminal able to receive eight million passengers during the six months permanence of the manifestation. The building of motor-ways and high ways to facilitate the access to Seville in the direction of Madrid and Malaga and the improvement of railway services with very fast trains.

Right on the Island of Certosa they are building a mastodontic bridge called Puente de Alamillo, which from the hospital area of St. Lazarus leads to the village of Camas, making a detour of the two public roads by Huelva. Other bridges which connect the historical centre to the Island of Certosa are situated one at the entrance to calle Calatrava, near the 'Macarena', another near the beginning of calle Banos, in the district of St. Vincent's church, still another between Plaza de Armas and Chapina (near the Museum of Fine Arts) and finally the Puente de las Delicias, near the homonymous walk.

Beside these bridges there is also the so called Puente del Centenario near the Docks of Bata, which possesses a light for 264 metres; supporting columns which are 105 metres high and 50 above the river Guadalquivir allowing the passage of boats bound for the port of Seville.

To reach the exhibition area a cableway has also been constructed. In addition a tower has been erected over 100 metres high on which a viewpoint has been set up from where visitors are able to enjoy a complete panorama of the area.

The surface of Expo-92 includes also an artificial lake, some nautical installations, a helioport, fifteen buildings assigned to places for shows, among which an Auditorium, a theatre for opera, some cinemas, sports establishments of all kinds, etc. One hundred and five gift and souvenir shops have been installed, one hundred and forty-three restaurants and bars, an overhead panoramic train, as well as green spaces with woods and gardens which contain over one hundred thousand plants.

The cost of the road network infrastructures has reached the staggering sum of 60,000 million dollars while the investments inside the exhibition area (without counting the pavillions of the various countries taking part have reached 1,000 million dollars. The centre of the Exhibition is situated in: **The Charterhouse of the Grottos.**

The Charterhouse of St. Mary of the Grottos (Cartuja de Santa María de las Cuevas) is a Carthusian monastery built in 1930 by the Archbishop Gonzalo de Mena.

The building is gothic style. When the Community of Carthusians disappeared, as a result of the suppression of the Orders in the 19th century, the complex was sold by the State and bought by an English man Charles Pickmann, who transformed the monastery into an important factory of majolica and artistic ceramics which enjoyed International fame with the trade name of "La Cartuja". To testify this industrial period remain some superb chimneys, true monuments of progress, opposite the Monastery of the Carthusians, which instead represents the historical past.

This monastery was chosen as the ideal place to house Expo-92 for its relationship with Columbus' family. Christopher Columbus was on very friendly terms with Brother Garricio, he studied ancient books of cosmography and navigation in the library of the monastery, to prepare for his last voyage and he deposited his documents and papers there so that they would not get lost during his absence due to his last voyage. On the death of Christopher Columbus in 1507 his body was buried in St. Ann's chapel, built at his expense, where he rested until 1536, the year in which his remains were transferred to the cathedral of the island of Santo Domingo. Finally there remains to be said that the first tree brought from America was an ombu that Fernando Columbus, the son of the navigator, planted in the

Monorrail EXPO 92.

Cartuja de Santa Maria de las Cuevas, Bridge of the ▶
fifth centenary; Torre Banesto; Bioclimatic Sphere.

On page 110: a suggestive view of the bridge called
La Barqueta.

Charterhouse and to be exact in the Patio de las Cadenas, where it still exists.

The main pavilions to have been installed in the exhibition area are: the **Royal and Government Pavillion**, reserved to receive personalities. The 15th century Pavilion, where, with models, documents and maps of the world at the time of the discovery is presented. There will be held film projections of documentaries and spectacles of folklore of the period.

The **Pavilion of the Discoveries** where will be held an exhibition of all the most important technical and scientific discoveries of our times.

The **Pavilion of Navigation** in which there will be presented the expeditions and geographical explorations as well as the progress of navigation up to the present day.

The **Pavilion of the Present and Future**, dedicated to the latest progress in the field of robotics, computer sciences, communication, artificial intelligence, genetic engineering, biology, astronomy and so on.

There are also the **Pavilions of ninety-six countries** among which the ex-Soviet Union, Germany, England, Austria, Italy, Denmark, Portugal, Finland, Norway, all the Latin American countries, Asiatic countries such as Korea, the Philippines, Oman, India, African countries like Guinea, Gabon, Camerun, the pavilions of the eighteen International organisations among which the International Olympic Committee, the world Organisation for Tourism, the Organisation members of the United nations, the Organisation of the Eastern Caribbean States, etc.

In the pavilions of the ninety-six countries will take place shows of typical products and of industry, but also cultural manifestations.

We have calculated that by the time if finishes, Expo-92 will have been visited by 18 million persons in a period going from April to October 1992. Once over, many of the buildings will be assigned to consulates for those countries who have built them, while there is a project to assign other installation to university centres, research centres and recreation centres.

114

FESTIVITIES AND FOLKLORE IN SEVILLE

There are two main festivities in Seville, both of International fame: Holy Week and the April Fair visited every year by hundreds of thousands of tourists who try to catch the real spirit of Seville.

HOLY WEEK

The processions of Holy Week in Seville are, at the same time, a religious act of external cult, which means celebrated outside the churches and an exhibition of all those arts that are connected with liturgy.

We can really say that, on the days of Holy Week, Seville is transformed into the richest museum in the world where it is possible to admire every kind of art. Representing sculpture there are various images, for carving the bas-reliefs of the groups carried in the procession, for gold-work the religious objects like medals, the silver engraved staffs which support the material in the shape of the baldachino, that covers the various sculptural groups, for embroidery the very rich decorations of the mantles of the Virgins, for the cloth the gold and silver threads of the hangings, baldachins and festoons, for wax art the candles and the church candles that illuminate the Virgins, for floral art the typical vases of flowers which can be found at the foot of the images.

Here we have a museum that fills us with wonder, touches our souls and upsets our senses. In front of one of these groups in processions, called *pasos*, we do not know whether to admire the baroque sculptures of the 17th century more or the delicate paintings and the silk embroidery or the small heads of the ivory angels or the gold embroidered velvet of the mantles themselves. The streets are literally overrun by processions for a whole week. Some set off at one o' clock in the afternoon and return to their churches at three o' clock the following morning.

At present there are 58 confraternities in Seville each with about a thousand brethren who dress as "nazareni" with a hood, tunic and cloak. The costumes of the various Confraternities have a particular symbolic significance on the basis of the colour, the tunic which may be leather, cloth or hemp. Also the embroidered coat of arms on the cloak has its significance, expressed by the ecclesiastical heraldry which indicated whether the confraternity has a pontificial or royal title o whether it has been founded by will of the Order of the Carmel or St. Francis or if it comes from a Military Order like that of the Knights of Malta or the Knights of the Holy Sepulcre.

On the previous pages, the procession of the Virgin and the characteristic «Nazarenos», who are part of one of the fifty-eight confraternities of Seville.

The procession of Christ.

The Confraternities carry two *pasos* in procession, one with Christ and another with the Virgin. The paso of Christ on the contrary to that of the Virgin is not furnished with a baldachin. Those of the confraternity who cover governing tasks carry a silver stick in their hands indicating their rank while the other bretheren carry a church candle. The penitent, whether bretheren or not bear one or more crosses as a symbol of pardon received, like a votive offering for the recovery from an illness or as penitence for the atonement for a wrong.

The paso is carried by the brethren called *costaleros* who load it onto their shoulders leaning the wood transverse called *trabajaderas* against the base of the neck. Each one of these *costaleros* bears a weight of approximately eighty kilos.

Some bretheren carry a *paso de misterio* in the procession, this means a sculptural group made up of several images such as *el Paso de la Sentencia* which represents the image of Christ, that of Pontius Pilate who is washing his hands in the water of a jar held by a coloured slave in the presence of scribes and judges of the Sunedrion, while he is protected by a group of Roman soldiers. We are dealing with a complete Gospel scene with life size figures of great plastic beauty.

There are many *pasos de misterio*. Among them stands out the Last Supper with Jesus and his twelve apostles. Christ's arrest and Exaltation of the Cross, the Deposition, etc. These works have been carried out from the 15th century up to the present by the greatest sculptors of religious subjects.

THE APRIL FAIR

Two weeks after the end of Holy Week, at the end of April, the Seville Fair is celebrated. It was created in 1847 as a cattle market, very soon the sellers and buyers installed nearby some little houses or open shops to refresh themselves in the shade and celebrate the concluded business by eating and drinking. And so the fair began to be animated by the cheerfulness of music and dancing, so much so, that, very soon, the enjoyment ended up by having more success than the real cattle market.

The so called *caseta de feria* (the fair house) is an annexe of the habitual house: in it there is furniture, mirrors, decorative objects which give it a folkloristic and gay characteristic. The floor of the little house is wood, so that it is possile to dance "Las Sevillanas", a typical dance that is performed in couples or groups of couples.

The most evocative spectacle is at midday, when the riders parade in their Andalusian costumes and the women dressed in ridinghabit when they are alone or dressed as gypsies when they are in a group, accompanied by a horseman.

The parade brings together in the area of the fair about a thousand harnesses and a hundred carriages of all kinds: drawn by one, two, three, four or five horses, passenger horses, pack horses, plough horses.

Country carriages, walking carriages, city carriages from a one horse carriage to a landau, a cabriolet, a tono, a sociable. As the parade of the horsemen and the carriages begins, they begin to toast in the houses too, they drink *Vino de Jérez* and *Manzanilla de Sanlucar*, the two classical wines of the fair.

In the evening the fair moves to the Plaza de la Maestranza, where the bull fight takes place. The Seville Fair bull fights are famous as the victory of the bull fighter means his professional consecration and a prestige that procures him contracts in all the arenas of Spain, France and Latin America.

The Plaza de la Maestranza is covered with a splendour of indescribable colours with the women in their flamenco costumes, embroidered baldachins and hangings from the stands, and the bull fighters in their very bright red, green or blue costumes with gold embroidery. At the end of the bull fight, after a short interval, they return to the Fair illuminated by thousands of lights and they toast again with wine, Sevillian dances and songs and it goes on all through the night until dawn.

The April Fair. The so-called Caseta de Feria (the Fair House) and the characteristic Sevillian dance.

◄ The April Fair, the «Portada» and the horse-riders in their folkloristic Andalusian costumes.

The Pilgrimage of the Rocío: a view of one of the carts, drawn by oxen, used to carry out the journey to the village of Rocío.

THE PILGRIMAGE OF THE ROCIO

The third of the great festivals of Seville is the *Romería* or Pilgrimage of the Rocío, which is celebrated in the month of June. Actually it is not a festivity which is exclusively Sevillian, since the Confraternity of Rocío from all over Spain take part and some coming from other countries. Without doubt most taking part are from Seville because of the nearness of the city to the village of Rocío.

Two Confraternities set off from Seville, one of Salvatore and the other Triana. These confraternities carry out the journeys as far as Rocío on horseback, each one with a few hundred horsemen and about ten carts drawn by oxen on which girls and women are seated.

The journey to Rocío lasts three days, during which they never stop walking, singing, dancing or drinking wine. In spite of this we cannot say that the religious part is less important as enjoyment is alternated by gathering and prayer. They sleep out in the countryside, on the carts or on the ground on a cover. At dawn the tambourines and flutes play again and Mass is celebrated under a tree. Soon after, the journey along trodden paths continues to reach the marshy plain of Rocío, near the village of Almonte. Here all the Confraternites gather more than a hundred, who have come across the country from various villages and towns. Each confraternity, in the open place of Rocío have their own dwelling where to refresh themselves.

In turn, each Confraternity celebrate their own Mass in the Sanctuary of Rocío and for two days the religious services follow one another continuously inside the church, while in the countryside the festivity is taking place with dances and songs. On Monday, at dawn, the Virgen del Rocío is carried in procession across the countryside and is taken back to its church of origin at midday. It is then that the Confraternities set off on their journeys back home along the same trodden paths in the burning June sunshine.

This Pilgrimage is a crowded spectacle, on the open spot of Almonte, during all the days on which it takes place. However the most interesting part is the outward and return journey which is, at the same time, a pilgrimage and folkloristic festivity which, without doubt, has no equivalent in all the Christian world.

THE OUTSKIRTS OF SEVILLE

THE MONASTERY OF SAN JERONIMO

It is situated in the suburb of St. Jerome, not far from the Cemetery of St. Ferdinand. It was founded in 1414 by some magnates of Seville with the name of San Gerolamo de Buenavista and is built in Gothic style. Later it underwent modifications in Renaissance style.

The church contained only one aisle and on the high altar the *image of San Jerónimo* was venerated, it is the work of the Italian sculptor Torrigiano, now it can be found it the Provincial Museum of Fine Arts of Seville.

Left of the sumptuous monastery there are only a few artistic remains, among which the splendid patio, which has been restored recently. It is worth a visit as it is one of the greatest Sevillian Gothic works.

THE RUINS OF ITALICA

The ruins of the city of Italica, built by Scipio after the defeat of the Carthaginians are fifteen kilometres from Seville, in the nearby village of Santiponce.

We do not know the exact area on which the city developed, however it must have been very large, judging at least from the extent of the Circus. It was estimated there was a population of over forty thousand inhabitants. Nevertheless only few streets inhabited by families of magnates have been brought to light. The richness of the buildings is shown by the great value of the mosaic pavements. Some of these mosaics, like those of the Four Seasons or the one representing the tiger hunting a deer can be considered among the most beautiful mosaic decorations of Roman antiquity.

Below the street runs a drainage system, a true work

◄ The crossing of River Quema.

A view of the ancient Monastery of San Jerónimo de Buenavista.

The ancient paved road leading to Italica.

The ancient Roman ruins in Italica; the town founded by the Scipions and the birthplace of the Emperors Traianus, Adrianus and Teodosius.

of art of engineering. The main building is the *Circus or Amphitheatre* whose area was used for the wrestling of the gladiators and fairs. The *cavae* are still visible where the wild animals were locked up, the passages (*vomitoria*) along which the public went in and out and the steps, which to a large extent have been preserved. The system of canalisation for the collection of rain water is provided by a big central cistern and this too is a great work of engineering.

Another public building of extraordinary interest is the *Theatre*, in which can be found beautiful sculptures and bas-reliefs representing actors, comedians and dancers.

The excursion to Italica is particularly recommended to lovers of Roman antiquity and it is indispensable in order to discover the true roots of the history of Seville.

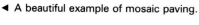
◄ A beautiful example of mosaic paving.

Some ancient Roman statues exhibited in the Museum and in the Amphitheatre of Italica.

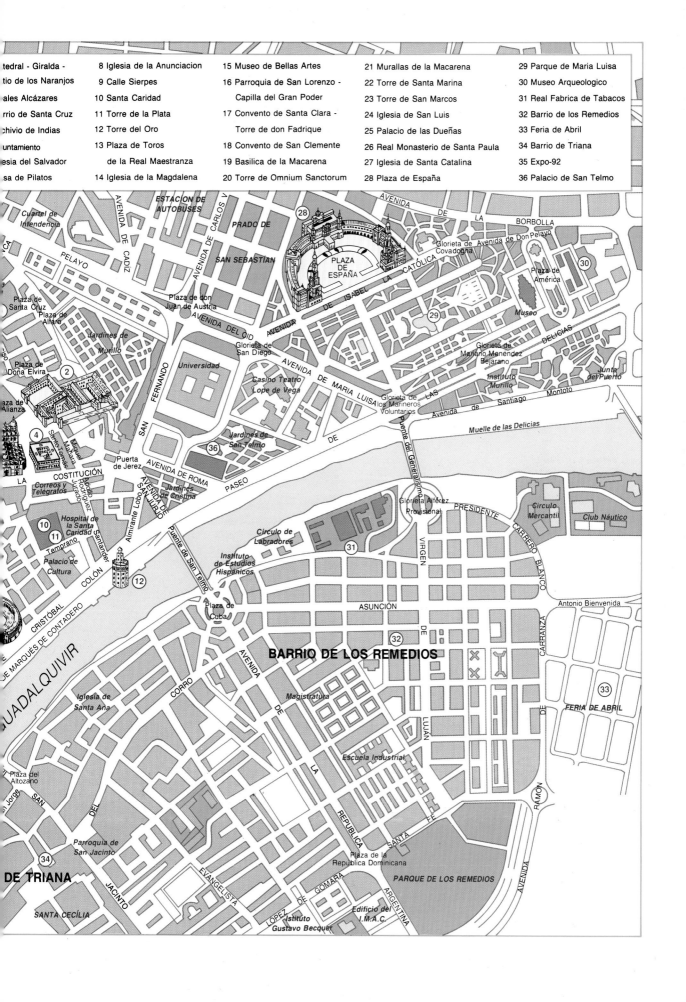

INDEX